IPR AND RESEARCH ETHICS

A GLIMPSE OF LAW AND ETHICS FOR ACADEMIC AND RESEARCH WRITING

DR. VITTHAL GORE - EDITOR

Dedicated to

My Beloved Parents

Late. Mrs. Manorama & Late Mr. Gangadharrao Gore

Contents

Foreword

I am happy to write this Foreword to the book titled *IPR and Research Ethics*, edited by Dr. Vitthal Gore. He has always been interested in academics and research activities ever since I know him as a Ph.D. scholar under my research supervision at Osmania University. He has contributed much, so far, to the online lectures, material on several relevant authors and subjects in the field of English literature.

The present book *IPR and Research Ethics* is also a similar attempt in bringing to bear sincerity and quality in English Studies in India. It is necessary that research scholars should have the right attitude and inclination towards their research. Research quality would improve certainly if they focus little more on the Ethics of research. Every year, so much research is going on in Indian Universities that innumerable number of books and research articles are getting published, but less attention is paid to the method and manner of research. In terms of quality, our scholars are not getting the requited recognition at the international level. This is happening because our research more often repetitive and falls short of originality. Now many Universities are taking care of the credentials of research by plagiarism check at their level. But individual scholar should also take enough care in maintaining quality and originality in their research. It is essential that each individual scholar should cultivate the habit of sincerity and right attitude of seriousness and honesty in their approach to research. The present book will be of use in widening the serious attitude of the scholars by bringing their attention to some of the issues involved in maintaining quality and originality of research. Especially, the knowledge of intellectual property rights and the seriousness of plagiarism in the research would ensure quality and sincerity in the research.

First of all, I congratulate Dr. Vitthal Gore for his one more industrious effort for editing a book on *IPR and Research Ethics*. All the articles solicited in this book are relevant to the title and show its genuine impulse of the topics. The segregation of all the chapters is also logical and seems to be of an expected sequence. This variety, right from intellectual property rights, plagiarism, research ethics, etc. have been legibly addressed by the respective contributors.

I hope the present book would meet this demand and will be of much help to the scholars and researchers across the universities in India and abroad. I compliment Dr. Gore in identifying the right area at the right time. I further hope that research scholars find this book useful and get the best by paying required attention to the contents of the book.

Dr. Biruduraj Yadava Raju
Retd. Professor of English and
Former Dean, Faculty of Arts,
Osmania University, Hyderabad, Telangana.
1 January 2023

Preface

The process of globalization has radically influenced the domain of research and publication all over the world. GATT which was renamed later as WTO i.e. World Trade Organization has compelled the member countries to accept the international laws in the respect of Intellectual Property Rights. Being a member country, India has also accepted the international norms in this respect and amended the intellectual property rights and brought the laws up to the international standards.

After certain amendments in the laws related to Intellectual Property Rights, research and publication scenario in India has gone through a sea change. The present book has become a reality by considering the need of the time. Thousands of research articles are being published in various domains of knowledge; universities are conferring research degrees at a large number but when it comes to our identity at international level for doing standard research in all domains remains questionable. University Grants Commission has been constantly looking into this aspect and encouraging faculty and researchers to undertake quality research by considering all the ethical practices in the domain. The present book has been edited in the view to provide an insight in to the realm of intellectual property rights and publication ethics hence it is titled as IPR and Research Ethics.

While soliciting research articles for this book, the faculty members working in different parts of the country have been invited to contribute their research articles. Sufficient time was given to all in order to write and process their articles for this book. The selected articles were meticulously reviewed and checked for plagiarism related issues. The online Plagiarism tools were used for the purpose of checking. The contributors have been intimated about their plagiarism reports; as and when needed, they were asked to make necessary additions, deletions and changes. The final versions of the articles have once again been reviewed and then finalized. All the contributors very patiently cooperated and completed entire process of reviewing and editing. All the necessary precautions have been taken in order to make it up to the mark.

The first chapter contributed by Dr. M. Raghvendra is titled as 'Importance of Intellectual Property Rights and Plagiarism: An Analytical Study'. It mainly focuses on the intellectual property rights with a legal perspective and makes us alert to be cautious about the law of the country. In addition, it talks about the threats of plagiarism as well.

The second chapter titled as 'Intellectual Property Rights and Plagiarism: A Researcher Perspective' is contributed by Janardhan V.P. The author deals with Intellectual Property Rights which boost up the innovative environment by giving recognition and benefits to creator or inventor whereas the lack of IPR and plagiarism awareness and its ineffective implementation may hamper the ethical, technical and societal developments of a nation. This paper presents an overview of the importance of Intellectual Property Rights and its different forms, regulations towards accessing the original works along with its effects.

'The Role of Plagiarism and Ethics in Research' by Basavaraja C. forms the third chapter of this book. Basavaraja interpreted the terms 'plagiarism' and 'research ethics'. He promotes the application of fundamental ethical principles to varieties of topics involving scientific research. He also advocated the guidelines of research which constitute to the quest for accurate, adequate and relevant knowledge.

In the fourth chapter titled 'Plagiarism: A Threat To Research Ethics' Rajesh Kale tries to convince readers that plagiarism is against research ethics and fundamental scientific principles. Plagiarism needs to be discarded from academics considering it as unethical, useless, unnecessary and meaningless. In view of the prevalence of plagiarism in the research community and its devastating effects on scientific progress, the present paper aims at surveying the concepts, causes and solutions to the issue of plagiarism.

Dr. Anjali Harangaonkar contributed the fifth chapter titled 'Research Ethics and Plagiarism'. For her research is creative and systematic work undertaken to upgrade the stock of knowledge which involves the collection, organization, and analysis of information to increase understanding of a topic or issue. Research involves the application of fundamental ethical principles to research activities which include the design and implementation of research, respect towards society and others, the use of resources and research outputs, scientific misconduct and the regulation of research. The author talked about the ethical dilemmas which are particularly problematic for editors and reviewers whose responsibilities include ensuring submissions meet journal standards.

Dr. Vitthal Gore, the editor of this book, contributed the sixth chapter tilted as 'Academic Research and Publication Ethics'. He looks at the entire academic research and publication scenario in our country. It is found that the research and publications have been a hidden treasure of the library shelves. While making comparison and contrast, this scenario with the American or European universities and a few very top-rated universities in the world; we realize our status, where do we really stand and why are we really lagging in the respect of academic research and standard publications. So, the present paper on Academic Research and Publication Ethics makes us aware about the research and publication ethics.

Dr. Sanjay Haibatpure contributed an article on 'Ethical Issues in Research: An Observation'. He has made a general overview of the realm of research and promoted the idea of ethical research as the demand of the modern world. The author insisted to adhere the ethical norms and bring out quality research and publication for building of the nation.

Dr. Divya Maheshwari's 'Online Educational Resources Must Safeguard the Core Credits of the Creators' forms eighth chapter of this book. This article focuses on the significance of online educational resources in all areas of the public domain, supporting an easy access to knowledge for learning, under an intellectual property license with the permission for free use or free from plagiarism, following the netiquette ethics. It emphasizes on plagiarism free research and the fact that the Intellectual Property Rights (IPR) should be properly protected for having much more significance in many areas such as research, innovation, economy as well as service sectors too.

Dr. K. Subbapriya's 'Challenges and Problems in Research Pertaining to Current Scenario in Tamil Nadu: A Practical Approach' deals with research as a meticulous process. In the current scenario, the research process involves various complications due to the new rules and regulations imposed upon the research and the researcher. This article ventures to trace the practical issues in the research process currently faced by researchers, examines the advantages and disadvantages of rules and regulations imposed by academic bodies, focuses on the lacuna in panel constitutions and finally tires to draw upon the conclusion that how certain steps could be taken to bridge those gaps. The paper encompasses the concept of research, ethics, plagiarism and the standard of research.

Dr. Sanjay Kulkarni's chapter on 'Higher Education in India: Itself a Research Potential Sector' makes an effort to present higher education sector as a separate realm of research. For him this field desperately needs a special attention of the researchers. India being as a vast country has a lot of diversity. In order to address the problems related to higher education, it's quality and research itself require special attention and faculty are expected to look into this arena of study as a potential area.

Ms. J.D. Sampale talks about plagiarism in her article titled *Basic Principles and Strategies to do a Plagiarism free Research'* Plagiarism encourages original research and stop the tendency of merely copying or presenting other's ideas. This paper mainly discusses the foundational principles of Plagiarism and the strategies to avoid this unethical practice while conducting research in various academic disciplines.

All together these solicited and edited articles have given an opportunity to the editor to edit and publish this book. It would not have come in to existence without the constructive contributions of all these authors. It gives me immense pleasure to present this edited book to all the faculty members, researchers and students. Hope it will help you in forming a right ethical attitude for research purpose and ethically publishing at the end.

I express my sincere gratitude to the Retired Professor B. Yadava Raju for writing foreword to this edited book. I am also thankful to all the contributors for their constructive role in bringing this book in to this comprehensive form. I also express my gratitude to all the office bearers of Bharat Liberal Education Society and Shri Havagiswami Mahavidyalaya Udgir for always encouraging for constrictive academic development. Last but not the least I also extend my heartfelt regards to Notion Press Chennai for giving me a platform to publish this book.

Dr. Gore Vitthal
1 January 2023

CHAPTER I

Importance of Intellectual Property Rights and Plagiarism: An Analytical Study

Dr. M. Raghvendra

Librarian (SG), Government First Grade College, Javanagondanahall, Karnataka.

Email: raghushira@gmail.com

IPR for Plagiarism Free Ehtical Practice

• • •

• • •

The definition of 'Intellectual Property' is someone's original and creative works which is protected by copyright, patent, trademarks and some trade secret laws. Further patents are divided into different ways, they are patent for inventions and copyrights for literary works, trade secrets and trademarks in the present globalizing world featured by multilateral trade, increasing accuracy and transparency have become more vulnerable to infringements. Thus, the prime thinking behind the IPR is that the writer must get his due credit, which will further support him to keep up the research and development. In India, science, technology, business methods and software are rapidly changing; they are protected by Intellectual Property Rights. However, all these matters and issues have to be analyzed afresh globally. Knowledge, information and communication technology factors play important roles in the global affairs today.

Many nations translate knowledge into social goods and wealth through research and development, creative ideas and innovations will lead the world in the twenty-first century. Research and development, innovation and time for grasping new knowledge have taken over cost to become significant determinants of the public perception of the market value of service and a product. With the knowledge-based economy advancing day by day, the existing management culture, and approach has to undergo a change. Specifically, in managing and understanding the knowledge-based assets such as designs, ideas and innovations. In this way human facilitates overall development of socio-economic and cultural aspects of the society must be supported, and the innovator or the creator must be rewarded by suitable legal protection for his intellectual creation. Thus matters related to evaluation, generation, exploitation and protection of intellectual property rights would become critically important across the world.

Importance of IPR in Contemporary Scenario

Intellectual Property Rights legally protect the rights of the creator or author who has transformed his/her ideas into property. In other words, legal rights are provided to stop others specifically pirates, imitators from taking credit of the original creator. Now, an invention which is an aggregation or duplication of known properties or traditionally known properties or conventionally known part or parts is not an invention. In other words, any discovery that does not show anything new and the knowledge which is already known and traditionally used is not considered as a 'new invention, so it cannot be patented.

Patent

A patent in general is a specific document, issued, by concerned governing authority which explains an invention and thereby creates a legal situation so that the patented invention can be taken advantage of manufactured, used, sold, and imported with the authorization of the owner of the patent.

Meaning of "Invention" is a solution to a particular problem in the field of technology and it associates to a process or a product. Patent confers in its protection in a limited time generally for 20 years.

Trademark

A trademark refers to any visible sign, design or a slogan that has the capacity to identify or individualize goods of a given enterprise and distinguishes them from those of others and thus it solely indicates its source of the product, but the consumer can trust in a given enterprise, not necessarily known to him by some trademarks under which the product is sold. In this way, the function of the trademark and its function of indicating the source cannot really be separated but they are interdependent. Any visible sign can differentiate goods and services of one enterprise from others are called as Trademark.

Trademark Rights are for words, names, slogans and designs are given for 10 years and are renewable for every 10 years with evidence of use in commerce.

Trade Secrets are the proprietorship rights which can possibly last for long; if the information is kept confidential. However, independent finding or development of the ownership information will then generate two or more free owners of the information, if they also maintain the information confidential.

Copyright

Copyrights and its laws are different branches of IPR that deals with the rights of intellectual authors / creators, various forms of creativity, not only in print form but also in other ways in which mind can perceive and imagination can afloat to work on. They are dramatic, artistic, musical and literary works and makers of films and sound recordings.

Copyright protection is the most important subject. 'Copyrights' are the special rights, which the laws confer on writers or creators to maintain their own rules and regulations for letting their intellectual property. The copyright of the author of a book to print copies is the oldest of all these special rights. This was the first copyright law, which was implemented in 1709 in the United Kingdom and is generally known as the 'Queen Anne's

Statute'. Copyrighted work cannot be translated, reproduced, exhibited, performed or adapted, distributed, communicated or broadcasted to the public without the consent of its author. This is what is meant by the phrase 'all rights reserved' found in many works.

Once a material is published anywhere in a member country of the Berne Convention, it becomes a copyrighted material and no separate registration is required. Copyright protection is automatic and ends throughout the author's lifetime plus 50 years after the death of author. However, in majority of countries, copyright protection ends longer than this minimum term. For example, in the USA and in countries of the European Union, copyright protection usually lasts during the life of the author plus 70 years after the author's death. However, it protects mere facts but not ideas.

Information which gets from internet is also an important subject matter of copyright, as it is available in public sphere. Information transferred and transmitted on internet may already be a copyrighted, but the situation becomes complicated because sometimes it becomes difficult to identify persons deal with the transaction of information the internet service provider, the user / person downloading the information / the content provider, and the bulletin board service provider. A collection of copyrighted works is transacted when the situation gets compounded.

Copyrights and Indian Constitution

India is committed to the system of multilateral trading being promoted under the aegis of WTO in which the scope of international law is being enlarged. Hence, there is an increase in the scope of Intellectual property Rights substantially. The judiciary has shown its different role to function in relation to Intellectual Property Rights as India has introduced many Intellectual property policies on par with the international policies. In these days, there is a need to change or modify the existing laws and introduce new provisions, but their long-term results have yet to be examined with other. While reviewing international policies or laws, the Indian courts haven't violated the established rules and regulations of international level. Even the Parliament of India has taken a lot of care in implementing internal laws, as it has not created any breach of international treaty and policy obligations which are reflected in the Article 51 of Constitution of India.

The judiciary has its prime responsibility to adjudicate Intellectual Property matters right from its genesis to the life cycle to end-result. All matters related to the utilization, creation, protection and enforcement of the Intellectual Property. On the one hand, the emerging Intellectual

Property Right outcomes, results and implications for the society fail in the domain of the Courts in India. Different Statutes like the Merchandise Act, the Indian Trade Act and Indian Patents Act have protected the created Intellectual Property. There are Quasi-Judicial Authorities exist under the above acts are Registrar of Trademarks and the Trademarks Appellate Board, Controller of Patents and Designs, Registrar of Copyrights and the Copyright Board. The utilization of Intellectual Property comprises some arrangements related to transfer, assignments, licensing, which require the norms as enshrined in the statutes like Indian Stamp Act, Transfer of Property Act and the Indian Contracts Act, etc.

Enforcing the intellectual property right is another important aspect, which is required for preventing others from unauthorized exploitation of protected intellectual properties, infringement/misappropriation of Intellectual Property as laid down in the laws of India is a crime and the statutes are there to ensure enforcement and infringements.

Plagiarism

Someone else's work, plan and ideas have been presented as your own work, plan and ideas into your work and pretended to show it as your own is called as plagiarism. It is unlawful to use someone's work as yours in every way with or without getting the approval of original author. Now, *plagiarism seems to be considered as a crime.* It ruins not only one's fame but also affects one's career. If it is not legal; it will not be allowed in any other field. You are the most important investment, hence don't steal. If you steal someone's work you will cheat yourself. It stops you from researching and developing your ideas and propositions. It is better to use sources specifically and properly instead of copying other's works.

While involving research project, you refer books, magazines and get information through internet, blogs, Wikipedia and others. Write down all the important points you want to use in your research work and elaborate them in your own words with meaningfully. If you've seen any sentence that sounds sharp to you, make some changes to it by adding some extra words of your own or change the sequence of words.

Importance and Impact of Plagiarism

Impact of plagiarism will give a better result to inventers, if anybody ignores it; the results will be horrible, it affects your work in every possible way, whether you're a student or a researcher, or a writer, plagiarism has its bad outcomes, as a student, it'll get you failed or expelled. If you use plagiarized content in your projects as a researcher and professional, it will cost you and consider as a cheater. It will cost your income but your future career too, your work won't get any recognition or appreciation and It will not be approved anywhere.

The content you make by copying someone else's ideas can never call as yours, it will not be considered original work and your work won't get any recognition, you can't rely on other's career for long. Your career will ruin and leave you a harmful effect if you are charges with plagiarism at once. It is considered unethical. It's not different from stealing, you'll see yourself as a plagiarist, and reputation will be lost.

Apart from the fact that plagiarism is a form of academic stealing, there are undoubtedly other reasons, owing to which researchers/ scholars should not plagiarize content. The prime aim of writer is to write his ideas and thoughts in his article to readers. Thus the readers connect with genuine ideas and thoughts of writer. The article fails to impress the readers as it loses its authenticity and trustworthiness. With the advent of technological advancements, it is easy to find duplicate content in articles by using plagiarism checker tool in these days.

Tips to avoid plagiarism

- A researcher has the best ideas to write an article earlier is the first step. He/she will not make delay that will have less time in the end to finish the article.
- As soon as you start the project or research, make sure to collect resources in abundance and develop your own ideas about your specific topic.
- Rephrase words while using the source. Quotes of the selected sources prove your answers. You will use the author's name, the title of the work when you quote in your article.
- The best way to avoid any claim of plagiarism is to mention the work you are using in your project.
- After completion of writing, review and edit the work meticulously. By using plagiarism checker software to check any plagiarised content. It will assist you to publish and without any identical content.

Conclusion

The entire paper encompasses the importance and impact of IPR and plagiarism, no doubt plagiarism seems like a very convenient way to work, it doesn't take much time and hard work, but one must be aware of the concept of plagiarism and its consequences, it takes you nowhere but behind the bar or may be charged with a hefty fine. It simply loses your importance and your work becomes unworthy and you won't raise highest stature by cheating others. Try to be more creative and use your ideas and create your work, make it unique and worthy. Tips and tricks that can help you to do plagiarism free work, in the same way IPR always stands with original works that makes everyone proud, so respect IPR and the concept of plagiarism which definitely helps in creating wonders.

References

Brogan, M. 1992. "Recycling ideas", College and Research Libraries, Vol.52 (5): 453–464.

Bruton, S.V. 2014. "Self-plagiarism and textual recycling: Legitimate forms and misconduct Accountability in Research", Policies and Quality Assurance, Vol. 21 (3): 17.

Butler, D. 2010. "Journals step up plagiarism policing", Nature, 466 (7303): 167.

Chandrasoma, R., C. Thompson, A. Pennycook. 2004. "Beyond plagiarism: transgressive and non-transgressive intertextuality", Journal of Language, Identity and Education, Vol.3 (3): 171–193.

De Voss, D., A.C. Rosati. 2002. "It wasn't me, was it?" Plagiarism and the web Computers and Composition, Vol.19(2), 191–203.

Khan, B.A. 2011. "Plagiarism: an academic theft". International Journal of Pharmaceutical Investigation, Vol8 (4): 255.

Pecorari, D. 2012. Textual plagiarism: How should it be regarded? Office of Research Integrity Newsletter, Vol.20 (3).

Rathod, S.D. 2012. Plagiarism: the human solution. Office of Research Integrity Newsletter, Vol. 20 (3).

CHAPTER II

Intellectual Property Rights and Plagiarism: A Researcher Perspective

Janardhan V. P.

Assistant Professor of English, Vani Sakkare Govt. First Grade College, Hiriyur, Karnataka.

Email: janivp1974@gmail.com

Plagiarism can take you behind the bars

Courtesy:https://static.igem.org/mediawiki/2009/6/60/ Ethics_IBB_Pune.png

• • •

• • •

In the era of globalization and advanced technology, it is most important to undertake research to derive great ideas, innovations and their results irrespective of every field. The characterization of intellectual property rights are associated with intangible assets owned by a person or company and protected against use without consent. Intangible assets refer to non-physical property; including right of ownership in intellectual property having many things right from patents, trademarks, industrial designs to recent software development.

Intellectual property rights and plagiarism are more important than ever in the present scenario, with all of the good the rise of the internet has done for the sharing of information along with their philosophies. It has become the fate of original authors that innovative works are easily extracted and incorporated into other works which have not truly identical works. They are definitely harmful to academic fraternity as well as economy and modernization of the country.

The law related to IPR (Intellectual Property Rights) are different from geographical disparities, at the same time most of the countries protecting their laws by implementing good governance against plagiarism to protect intellectual rights towards the original authors, whereas they also care their economy in terms of investment in academic and research, patents, copyrights, trademarks, etc. will be thoroughly kept under tight laws. In the field of higher education and research and in the trade and commerce, innovative ideas will be truly honoured with name and fame, that has to be proudly protected irrespective of countries with international cooperation and monitoring, few international bodies like UNESCO, UNICEF and UNO have maintained international standards to protect copy right laws at global level. It also referred to the particular groups that are looking for trademarks, inventions and patents which have separate governance in their respective countries to protect them from malpractices.

The problems related to identity, rectification, manipulation and violation of intellectual property rights and its laws are censoriously very much significant across the globe. Many countries have created a manifestation of severe punishment against violation of IPR law, a few countries have just initiated law against IPR but not effectively implemented to the grass root level, which is also a big failure and incapability to handle the issues related copyright law.

Recent technologies have motivated us to protect the law at the same time it also enables many users to approach in a back door access and provoke violation of the IPR laws. At the end of the day, it is important how effectively the laws against the offense are implemented. It is equally important that the matter whether it is developed or developing country how you have to react to it is all about; in India law against IPR is very strong. Plagiarism is an offense but still smooth corner kind of nature for the victims somewhere motivating them to violate the law again and again.

Significance of IPR and Plagiarism

At the global level, evolution of IPR was very interesting and it initiated in the 19th century itself. The fortification of Industrial property was long back in the 18th century at London. The patents, trademarks and industrial designs are covered under the resolution, after many years India has joined the treaty called "Paris Convention". Literary and artistic works are also part of the agreement under the law, later The General Agreement on Tariff and Trade (GATT) has come to existence to protect IPR. Till the 19th century, then World Intellectual Property Organization (WIPO) initiated to protect the intellectual rights in 1960. Finally the World Trade Organization (WTO) came in to existence in the year 1995 to protect and implement strict laws in support of intellectual rights.

As industrial revolution started in the middle of 19th century; the developed countries have implemented their own registered bodies to look after IPR, by seeing all these developments UN has initiated a body called Trade Related aspects of Intellectual Property Rights (TRIPS) in 1995 and India also become the member of this body. After this development, India has initiated with a few commissions to look into the IPR and its implementation through strict laws against the violation of IPR.

The implementation of IPR in developing countries has positive growth predictions and especially technological inclusions to the IPR laws have showed tremendous involvement in implementing effective and efficient regulations to protect IPR in a better way. Whereas deprived countries have not shown much interest in order to implement laws against IPR, but the issues connected to IPR and plagiarism fortification and manipulation of IPR certainly become more serious and significant round the globe.

There are three different types of Intellectual Property Rights (IPR) as defined by World Intellectual Property Organization (WIPO) Patents for new discoveries, Copy Rights for literary and creative works and Trademarks for different symbols and logos.

'Plagiarism' is formally summarized as a kind of burglar concert of another person's ideas, inventions, intellectual works, original works of authorship, slogans, designs using them as your own without proper acknowledgement or without his\her permission of true owner or it can also be defined as copying others work without taking permission of the original author.

Indian Perspective

In India copy right violation is not officially permitted, the original ideas or works can be implemented to next level by acknowledging the original author, but ignoring is purely against law, the replications and outlying variations of any others work also tends to violation of IPR so in this context especially in academic environment many changes have been recorded, that to in advancement of technology stealing has reached to its next level; at the same time identifying the same is also implemented in a better way by using the advanced technology.

India has seen drastic changes in terms of implementing IPR laws. The very first step was Patent Act which came in 1970. It was a kind of support and protection against misuse of Patents. Then after many years the same act first amendment was done in 1999 which includes additional wings to protect laws. The second amendment was done in 2002 to elaborate and related things covered under the law. It came into force in India on 20 May 2003 which is almost the secure one against the IPR. For designs in India a few major steps have been taken up i.e. Design Act of 1991 which was then amended with the New Design Act 2000. Similarly for trade mark, the old act was Trade and Merchandise Marks Act 1958. The new act is Trade Marks Act 1999; it came into force on 15th September 2003. Likewise for copyright, many acts have been implemented at different stages like the first Copy Right Act 1957; the Act was amended in 1983, 1984, 1992, 1994, 1999. The most recent amendment was done in 2012.

International Cooperation

India became member of WTO long back and stands along with international trade standards by signing IPR and trade related issues. A few treaties which India has signed are as follows.

Budapest Treaty:

It is one of the important international treaties; it is mainly concerned with the recognition of deposit of microorganisms for patent procedure.

Paris Convention:

This treaty mainly deals with properties related to industries and trade.

Berne Convention:

This treaty is the landmark in the history of IPR, this agreement specially protects the intellectual literary, scholarly and artistic works.

Washington Treaty:

This is a kind of agreement related to integrated circuits and electronics designs.

Nirobi Treaty:

It is an agreement on protection of Olympic Symbol and Sports

Marakesh Treaty:

It deals with published literary works for visually impaired and person with physical challenge.

Recently in 2020, the central union of India has signed agreements with different countries related to WIPO on international classification system.

Actual Problems in India

In India the effective implementation of IPR and law against plagiarism is really good and providing justice but some legal issues have been disturbing them, for instance a few amendments are not allowing people to go beyond explorations like article 3(d) and Compulsory licensing for some research; one should have license to do some research i.e. it will not allow copyrights to original forms of a recognized component without any healing properties. Similarly, in case of foreign investors who wanted to implement any new technology definitely they have to think about misconduct of compulsory licensing to duplicate their products it's been a great impact on India-EU FTA negotiations.

India has many consolidated problems with the other countries when it comes to international standards because as usual 'Priority Watch List' of USTR for suspected desecration of IPR, which leads to many problems. The developed countries have their own way of dealing with it and executing their laws strictly; whereas a country like India has to think twice before implementing these, foreign investment will be disturbed, international inflow of money in trade and business will be affected; so soft corner about the culprit leads many issues.

Data privacy in our country has become common question to ask; it is not safe as bureaucracy is in dilemma whether to follow government rules or the super power ruling bypassing government. On the other hand, proper infrastructure and technology to protect highly secured data is always a question. More over developing countries like India doesn't care for commercial use of tested data, specially tested and submitted to government for crucial purpose.

There are many lists available to make a note that our country in the name of development is not willing to implement strong Law against IPR and plagiarism which leads many distractions in the of academics and research, trade and business, art and artistic works.

Conclusion

A vision can definitely set a platform to respect all intellectual works across the country IPR and plagiarism has to protect in a most prioritized way then only progress will check their proximity to its level the best, new ideas, innovative technologies anything new always be supported for better experience in day to day life, without inventions no progress and you can't expect any development, hope a day will come to implement to protect IPR and Plagiarism in a better way as developed countries have done it in a healthier way to support innovations and new ideas, irrespective of the country an international law could be implement to save and protect IPR and plagiarism around the globe.

References

Bharat, M. (2014). *Introduction to Intellectual Property Rights*, Himalaya Publications, Bangalore, p. 16-21.

Digvijay Singh, K. (2017). *IPR and its importance in Academic Development*, Ess Publications, New Delhi, p. 54-63.

Ganguly Gyan, S. (2010). *Intellectual Property Rights*, Ashok Publication, New Delhi, p. 41-57.

Zofar Mohammed, L. (2009). *IPR and Public Policy*, Himalaya Publications, Bangalore, p. 71-82.

Mohammed Zabiulla K. (2007). *IPR and Public Development*, Rudra Publications, Mumbai, p. 101-114.

CHAPTER III

The Role of Plagiarism and Ethics in Research

Basavaraja C.

Assistant Professor and Head, Department of English, Government First Grade College for Women, Chitradurga. Karnataka.

Email: sscbasavaraja@gmail.com

Be ethical, don't voilate IPR

Courtesy: https://pix4free.org/assets/library/2021-02-07/originals/copyright_infringement.jpg

• • •

• • •

In research activities and projects, the terms plagiarism and research ethics have been playing an important role. Before notification of the norms about plagiarism by the UGC, there were some researches done in various disciplines did not strictly follow the plagiarism and research ethics because the percentage of plagiarism was higher than acceptable today. If the researcher has undertaken his/her research work, he/she will have given clear applications of his/her findings in the research. If the researcher has plagiarized the text or image or something else in research, loses its originality. The plagiarism is the violation of conduct, ethics of research and so on. The guidelines of plagiarism and research ethics are very essential in these days; as a large number of aspirants are involved in researches as their passion and get employments and career advancement schemes in colleges and universities.

Plagiarism

According to Merriam-Webster's Online Dictionary 'Plagiarism' means "to steal and pass off (the ideas or words of another) as one's own: use (another's production) without crediting the source [... or] to commit literary theft: present as new and original an idea or product derived from an existing source."

In 'Plagiarism', a researcher is presenting someone's words, sentences, texts, ideas or piece of information as his/her own, without mentioning a proper citation.

'Plagiarism' is a kind of academic dishonesty and a kind of theft.

'Plagiarism' is an act of fraud. It steals somebody's work and uses it in their work.

Research Ethics

The term, 'Research Ethics', generally includes a wide variety of norms, values and institutional arrangements which help to constitute and regulate scientific activities.

The meaning of 'Research Ethics' comprises the application of fundamental ethical principles to varieties of topics involving scientific research. It is built on trust.

'Research Ethics' is a codification of scientific morality in practice. 'Research Ethics' has specific and basic rules and regulations for researchers. Rules and regulations are structured on general ethics of science, just as general ethics is structured on the context of morality of society at large.

It also gives its meaning as a method, procedure or perspective for deciding how to act and analyze complex problems and issues.

The term 'research' covers doctoral research fellows and all levels of students who are involved in different works. The norms of research usually cover research and how research deals with various activities i.e. dissemination of research, teaching, management of institutions and experts advise. Research ethics focuses on the disciplines that study standards of conduct, such as philosophy, theology, law, psychology or sociology.

Importance of Research Ethics

The research covers doctoral and post-doctoral research, students' research activities and projects, etc. The norms of research usually cover dissemination of research, teaching, management and expert's advice. Research ethics intends to maintain disciplines which include theology, psychology, philosophy, sociology and so on.

Research ethics promotes the aims and goals of research, such as knowledge, truth, and avoidance of error. It involves a great deal of cooperation and coordination among many people in different disciplines and institutions, ethical standards promote the values that are essential to collaborative work, such as trust, accountability, mutual respect, and fairness. The ethical norms like authorship, copyright and patenting policies, data sharing policies, and confidentiality rules in peer review are designed to protect intellectual property interests while encouraging collaboration. The ethical norms help to ensure that researchers can be held accountable to the public.

It also applies to types of researches such as public and private. The guidelines of researches constitute to the quest for accurate, adequate and relevant knowledge. The researchers have maintained in the above aspects especially originality, openness, trustworthiness and academic freedom and so on. The guidelines also regulate the research community about their integrity, impartiality, criticism and accountability. The relationship between researchers and the people whom they interact is an important one. While research is going on, the researcher has given a lot of respect, maintained confidentiality and free and informed consents from people whom they wanted to do research. Finally, many of the norms of research ethics promote a variety of other important moral and social values, such as social responsibility, human rights, and animal welfare, compliance with the law, health and safety.

Importance of Plagiarism Free Research

- Avoiding Plagiarism supports researchers and students to write unpublished and original work.
- It helps researchers to produce valid information.
- It creates motivation among researchers and students to write original write reports.
- Plagiarism also creates fear among researchers while they are undertaking researches.
- By avoiding Plagiarism researchers and students can express their new ideas that are useful to a large number of people.
- It creates a space for those who are interested in research activities.
- In these days plagiarism has created as an obstacle for those who are involved in stealing information from others.
- Plagiarism free researches have attracted a large number of readers across the globe.
- Plagiarism free dissertations are submitted by researchers to universities which are recognized as the highest rank holders in excellence.
- Plagiarism free research reflects the conduct and ethics of the researchers.

In this way, plagiarism free research activities have got a pivotal role in producing reliable researches in universities from researchers and students.

Types of Plagiarism

We have to various forms of plagiarism, in which researchers and students reuse entire document, make a copy and paste and rewrite entire paragraph or content as it is, without giving proper credit to the original authors.

1. **Word to Word Quotation:** In which writers, researchers and students rewrite the word to word quotations without including their independent ideas and thoughts in their works, even they haven't been given clear acknowledgement to the original authors.
2. **Paraphrasing:** The researchers and students are involved in changing the order of sentences by altering the words in paragraphs without giving proper acknowledgement to the authors.
3. **Mosaic Plagiarism:** Various phrases, ideas, opinions, thoughts from different sources to create patch work of other researchers' works

without proper citations is called mosaic plagiarism.

4. **Inaccurate Citation:** While citing sources, researchers prepare lists of sources (i.e.in bibliography) footnotes, in- text references about primary source and secondary sources.

5. **Failure to Acknowledge Assistance:** It refers to get the assistance from fellow students, laboratory technicians and other external sources. It has not referred to the supervisors, tutors and ordinary proof readers. This leads the comfortable changes about methods, approaches and content among researchers and students.

6. **Using material from Professional Agencies:** Here the researchers and students undertake their researches independently in their knowledge, intellectual training and development. They don't use any piece of material that has been published and produced by the agencies and other people.

7. **Self-Plagiarism:** The researchers and students are using a piece of material that they had already used in their previous works. The readers who want to get new one and new ideas.

8. **Global Plagiarism:** In which the researchers and students write entire work that was already written by someone else. This form is considered as one of the severe forms of plagiarism.

How to avoid Plagiarism

Researchers are usually writing ideas and information of secondary resources in their research. While using secondary materials, the researchers are expected to follow the plagiarism rules that are formed by the UGC. Sometimes it is very essential to use the same materials when the researchers have followed certain rules to rewrite the same information. If the researchers want to include words, phrases, sentences, paragraphs, passages and ideas of others' works, they must use them as quotations. They will lucidly cite all quotations when they quote words, phrases, sentences, paragraphs, passages and ideas of others' works.

Secondly the researchers do express the same ideas, phrases, paragraphs and passages taken from secondary sources by summarizing completely in their own words. If researchers are substantially indebted to a particular argument in the formulation of their own, they should make this clear both in footnotes and in the body of their texts according to the agreed conventions of the discipline, before going on to describe how their own ideas develop or diverge from this influence. Sometimes it is not necessary to give references for facts that are common knowledge in their discipline. If they are unsure as to whether something is considered to be common knowledge or not, it is safer to cite it anyway and seek clarification. They do need to document facts that are not generally known and ideas that are interpretations of facts. The knowledge in various disciplines has been developed cumulatively as a result of years of research, innovation and debate by researchers and other writers, hence, they need to give credit to the authors of the ideas and observations when they use. Not only does this accord recognition to their work, it also helps them to strengthen their arguments by making it clear the basis on which they make it. Moreover, good citation practice gives readers an opportunity to follow up their references, or check the validity of their interpretations.

Ethical lapses in research can significantly harm human and various disciplines, students, and the public. In short research ethics includes honesty, objectivity, integrity, openness, carefulness, responsible publication, confidentiality, respect for intellectual property, non-discrimination, legality, competence and others.

Thus, plagiarism and research ethics have made a pivotal role in undertaking research and changing scenario of the society and institutions. They produce an excellent works that will recognize institutions at national and international levels. They have supported to produce reliable researches and such are very useful for society and nation. They also help researchers who have gained a lot of respect from different fields.

References

Anand Agricultural University. Web.15 September 2021 http://www.aau.in/sites/default/files/ Unit%203%20RESEARCH%20AND%20RESEARCH%20ETHICS%20.pdf

University of Oxford. Web. 15 September 2021 https://www.ox.ac.uk/ students/academic/guidance/skills/plagiarism

Oxford University Press. Web. 13 September 2021. https://www.encyclopedia.com/social-sciences/dictionaries-thesauruses-pictures-and-press-releases/research-ethics

"Plagiarize." Merriam-Webster Online Dictionary. Merriam-Webster Online. 13 September 2021. http://www.merriam-webster.com/ dictionary/plagiarize

https://www.plagiarism.org/article/what-is-plagiarism Web. 16 September 2021

CHAPTER IV

Plagiarism: A Threat To Research Ethics

Rajesh Mahesh Kale

Assistant Professor, Department of English, Santosh Bhimrao Patil Arts, Commerce & Science College, Mandrup, M.S.

Email: rajeshkale909@gmail.com

Say No To Plagiarism

Courtesy: www.1.bp.blogspot.com/_RzmIlSwLsTQ/S_Ilc-Wdd0I/AAAAAAAAASo/3KACpa3oV_U/s1600/plagiarism.gif

• • •

• • •

In the last two decades, with the advancement of ICT, various websites provide scholarly articles, the copy paste tools and loads of pre-fabricated research papers, has made an increase in plagiarism in research. The author of a book, paper, poem or a scientific passage, after hours of contemplation and writing about a subject, puts to paper the sweet fruit of years of the rigorous efforts. As such, the plagiarist not only steals the fruit of such efforts but registers all that painstaking work to his own name also. Plagiarism is not a new phenomenon, it is hundreds of years old, but, due to the progress in information technology, it has now acquired new and different face as compared to the past. Plagiarism was almost a rare phenomenon until the last century, but it has spread across the world in recent years and has created a sense of fear and worry in the academic community. In the past, there were a few genuine researchers who used to produce authentic research and some of them would write not more than a couple of papers in their lifetime. Previously, there were just a few journals and they had very strict reviewing principles at work. Today, however, a number of researchers, journals and papers has really increased unimaginatively. There is no problem with the increase in the number of research papers but the main problem is the peer-reviewing of the papers. It is obviously expected from a reviewer that he should have a thorough knowledge in the subject of a paper. But, given the large number of papers to be reviewed, are there enough specialists to review the papers? No reviewer can claim that he/she has studied all the specialist papers in the area of knowledge and this paves the way for some plagiarists to take disadvantage of this situation.

Ben Jonson was the first one to sue the term plagiarism in the early 17th century. It was hard for authors to safeguard their writings before devising the copyright laws. But as plagiarism increased in the 18th century and copyright laws were clearly defined and devised by the middle of the century, plagiarists faced a change in the public opinion and strong ethical viewpoints towards plagiarism.

Definitions and Conceptual Note

1. Wilson Mizner states that "when we steal an idea from one author, it will be called plagiarism, but when we do it from a few authors, it is called research".
2. The word plagiarism comes from the word "plagarius", meaning kidnapper, robber, misleader, and literary thief".

3. Plagiarism usually refers to stealing ideas or words that are higher than the level of public knowledge.
4. In Webster's Dictionary, a plagiarist is defined as "One who plagiarizes, or purloins the words, writings, or ideas of another, and passes them off as his own; a literary thief" and plagiarism as "taking someone's words or ideas as if they were your own"
5. The University of Liverpool defines plagiarism as the "use of materials from unacknowledged sources or direct quotation of materials from documented references without acknowledging that the words have been taken verbatim from those references"
6. Plagiarism is an unethical activity in scientific writing. For something to be called plagiarism, it needs to be a serious deviation from normally accepted behavior of the relevant scientific community which is to be done consciously and deliberately and should be proven with rock-hard evidence. Plagiarism can occur in different forms: stealing ideas and stealing some parts of texts. Self-plagiarism occurs when an author uses his or her own previously published work without acknowledging it
7. Self-plagiarism may be defined in three different ways:

    a. publishing a paper which overlaps another paper without any acknowledgement;
    b. compressing a large paper into a few smaller papers and publishing them independently, called salami slicing and
    c. Republishing the same work.

Duplicate or redundant publication occurs when there is an overlap, without acknowledging it, between the two papers in terms of their abstracts, hypotheses, arguments, and data or findings. This may include an overlap with other writers, their findings or their samples. The following are some examples of republishing: publishing data which has been published before, reusing data in terms of figures and tables in later publications, publishing larger papers using previous smaller papers, publishing using the same data in two different papers, and publishing the same paper under two different titles.

Republishing is certainly unacceptable as it is done in a deceptive way. If editors, reviewers and end readers notice the overlap between different papers, they should make the right decision about it. Duplicate publication is deceptive and involves three major problems: it is unethical, it wastes data and resources and it has adverse impact on future research decisions. Editors and readers of a published report want to make sure that they are dealing with new and important data, and may wrongly be persuaded to think so, while this is not the case. Duplicate or redundant publication misleads the readers and reduces the credibility of the journal as well as its ability to attract quality papers. Duplicate publication wastes resources by wasting the time which could be allocated to other papers.

Most academic researchers agree that plagiarism is a serious problem in the ethics of publication. Plagiarism is seen to appear in different forms: stealing ideas and stealing texts (verbatim plagiarism). Plagiarism is no doubt an example of malpractice in research. Stealing part of the text and rephrasing it is a severe problem in the literature and humanities.

Plagiarism is attributing someone else's original work to yourself without attributing credit to the authentic author, copying other's ideas or words without giving the credit to the source, not using quotations in quotation marks, giving the wrong information about a reference, changing the words while keeping the structure of a sentence from another source without acknowledging it, and copying a large number of ideas or words from other sources without due acknowledgement to the original.

According to Maurer, Kappe, and Zaka another explanation of plagiarism numerates the ways of plagiarizing in the following way: "'copy-paste' which means verbatim copying of words; plagiarizing ideas, which consists of using an idea or a concept which is not commonly known to others; rephrasing, which means changing the grammatical structure, by using synonyms, reordering the original sentences, or rewriting the same content in different words; artistic plagiarism, which means presenting others' works using a different medium such as voice, text or image; plagiarizing codes, which means, using other programs' codes, algorithms and functions without the right permission or referencing, using expired or neglected links, adding quotation marks or other referencing signs without providing the right referencing information or updating links to sources, inappropriate use of quotation marks, failure to recognize the quoted parts of a text, incorrect referencing, i.e., adding incorrect referencing information or references which do not exist and plagiarism in translation, which consists of translating a text without giving reference to the original text". With regard to the intentions, plagiarism can be divided into two types. The first type is intentional plagiarism in which the author is completely aware of the act of plagiarism and is willing to perform it. The second type of is unintentional plagiarism where a person plagiarizes unknowingly due to lack of awareness and lack of skill in writing. The latter type is unintentional and this could be prevented.

In yet another classification, plagiarism can be divided into four categories:

1. "Casual plagiarism, which occurs because of lack of awareness of plagiarism, or insufficient understanding of referencing or citation;"
2. Unintentional plagiarism, happens due to the wide amount of knowledge in the scientific area, a person may unknowingly present ideas similar to those of others;"
3. Intentional plagiarism, where a person deliberately and knowingly copies part or all of somebody else's work without giving credit to them; and
4. Self-plagiarism, which consists of reusing one's own published work in a different form with acknowledging it".

Factors of Plagiarism

According to Ashworth, the concept of plagiarism is not clear enough so much so that some students are afraid of unwitting plagiarism while putting to paper what they take to be their own ideas. Studies show that researchers and teachers have different perspectives of plagiarism. Flint, Clegg, Macdonald opine that for some teachers, there are some definitions which are influenced by higher values such as the copyright, personal efforts and unity in the academia. According to Auer and Krupar, the uncontrolled availability of online databases, with all its benefits, has also impacted a rapid growth in plagiarism. Some factors affecting the attitudes of young researchers toward plagiarism are ignorance, lack of personal involvement in their studies, situational ethics, and lack of consistent styles among various disciplines. Dordoy points out some of the most important factors influencing plagiarism which include unethical promotions in respective profession, laziness or carelessness, preferring easy to access materials on the Internet, deliberate unawareness of rules and unwitting plagiarizing. Some other factors causing plagiarism are to achieve an academic degree or promotion to higher scales, researchers do not give utmost commitment to the learning process, instead they thrive upon practicing plagiarism in research activities. Besides, the life style of researcher, social and family pressures, etc. make researchers try to achieve the best results with the least efforts and in the least time. In the past, students used to go to libraries, retrieve information and had to retype it while today with the rapid development of the Internet, this painful and time-consuming process has transformed and the computers with internet browsing and skill to search with correct keywords have made plagiarism and cheating easier than never before.

Dellavalle, Banks and Ellis are of the opinion that in Indian universities, there is a huge of pressure on teachers and researchers to publish so that if they do not publish in journals with high impact factors or indexed journals, they will not get promoted even if they have high potential. This situation can aptly be represented with the saying "Publish or Perish." Therefore, many scholars make ethical practices under the pressure to get promotion and rush to the publishing journals.

Robert Harris takes students' looking for short cuts, their low interest in the research subject, their low planning skills, mismanagement of time, lack of skills in scientific writing and their interest in ignoring regulations as some of the reasons why students take to plagiarism.

The following are among the most important reasons why researchers plagiarize:

1. Ignorance towards research ethics: Some students plagiarize without intentions, many a times, they are not familiar with proper ways of inserting quotes, paraphrasing, citations and referencing.
2. Values/attitudes towards research: Some researchers find no reason why they should not plagiarize or they do it because of professional and social pressure.
3. Defiance: To some researchers, plagiarism is one of the tangible ways of showing dissent and expressing intentional disrespect for authority. They regard the task as neither challenging nor vital.
4. Temptation and opportunity: It are both easier and more tempting for researchers to plagiarize as information becomes more accessible on the Internet and web search tools make it easier and quicker to find and copy.
5. Lack of deterrence: To some researchers the profits of doing plagiarizing outweighs the risks, particularly if they think that there is little or no chance of getting caught and there is little or no punishment if they are caught.

Detecting Plagiarism

The task of detecting plagiarism is difficult and this makes the act of plagiarism a threat to the healthy research culture. Often plagiarism is detected and discarded by learned reviewers who possess up-to-date skill and knowledge in their own specialist filed.

The following sections include some of the methods that can be used by researchers to detect plagiarism.

1. General overview of the content: the academic staff should assess the structure of sentences, grammar and idioms used in the works. They have to examine the assignments which are lower or higher than the abilities of researcher.

2. Searching online bookstores: the online book stores help the academic staff to decide whether the students have mentioned the right dates of publications or whether the sources which have been used were appropriate to the content of their writings.

3. Search keywords: searching keywords in any available search engines on web is yet another tool in the hands of academics to find plagiarism. Today's searching technology makes it possible to search a whole text, if the work is plagiarized, instantly the similar content will be shown on the web.

4. Using plagiarism services: there are many tools, software applications and web sites which can help in detection of the plagiarized texts. Most of these tools use correlation techniques to detect similarities between texts and documents. Very few of these applications are free of cost and they can be used very effectively for English texts. There are some similar methods; however, those can be used in other languages also. The Glatt plagiarism service, for example, is a computer application which does not use correlation techniques. It keeps on deleting every fifth word in a text suspected of plagiarism and the author of that paper is asked to fill in the missing words. For Harma and Singh, if the author fails to fill in 77% of the missing words then it can be concluded that the work is most probably plagiarized. Wcopyfind is a free application on the Internet which can be used to detect plagiarism. This software examines a group of document files to compare their contents.

5. There are other online tools such as http://turnitin.com, http://ithenticate.com and http://www.crossref.org to detect plagiarism from texts, but these tools can examine the papers indexed in MEDLINE

only. This area of study has been attended to by Turnitin and Safe Assign in the last 10 years. Kohler and Weber-wulf carried out a study in 2010 on 47 systems of direct plagiarism detection and concluded that only 5 of them were to some extent useful.

Approaches to detect plagiarism

There are three approaches to detect plagiarism from any given text. The most common approach is by comparing the document against a number of other documents on a word by word basis. The second approach is by taking a characteristic parts and paragraphs and just doing a search with any search engine like Google, Bing etc. And the third is Stylometry in which the detection is done by style analysis of a given text. The plagiarism reports generated by computer applications cannot be simply relied on. Sometimes detecting plagiarism becomes very difficult, especially when rephrasing has occurred, when non-electronic sources have been used and when there is a deliberate shift of language between the original document and the plagiarized one. Although comparing abstracts is also a good way to detect plagiarism, a comparison of the full texts will render better results.

Strategies to Avoid Plagiarism

1. Adherence to the strict rules and instructions for authors provided by the journal.
2. Acknowledge the contributions of others and the source of ideas and words, whenever necessary, regardless of whether the content is paraphrased or summarized.
3. Use of verbatim content should be enclosed in quotation marks.
4. Acknowledge the original sources used in the writing.
5. While paraphrasing, understand the material thoroughly and use your own words.
6. If you are in doubt about whether or not the concept or fact is common knowledge, give reference of it.
7. Make sure to give references and cite references accurately.
8. If the results of a single extensive study are best presented as a cohesive whole, they should not be used into multiple separate articles.
9. When submitting a manuscript for publication containing research questions/hypotheses, methods, data, discussion points, or conclusions that have already been published or disseminated in a significant manner (such as previously published as an article in a separate journal or a

report posted on the Internet), alert the editors and readers. Editors should be informed in the covering letter, and readers should be alerted by highlighting and citing the earlier published work.

Conclusion

Ethical problems in research are rapidly increasing and have become one of the controversial issues in higher education in the country. These problems have also been reflected in culture and media more recently. The explosion of information and communication technology, competition between researchers, rapid growth of knowledge, flood of research journals, lack of awareness of plagiarism and different understandings of it, etc. have contributed to the prevalence of plagiarism in the research community. Some institutions focus on detecting and oppressing malpractices in research while others concentrate on preventions and teaching the right research behavior. Extreme stress on detecting plagiarism has enormously increased the mechanism of data retrieving systems in recent years, but these are neither effective enough, nor the best solutions to prevent plagiarism from research. Effective prevention through proper awareness at the right time, appropriate interaction between research supervisors and researchers and devising appropriate policies for this purpose can serve to be the possible means of tackling plagiarism.

References:

Auer NJ, Krupar EM. Mouse Click Plagiarism: The role of technology in plagiarism and the librarian's role in combating it. Library Trends. 2001; 49 (3):415-32

Austin MJ, Brown LD. Internet plagiarism: Developing strategies to curb student academ48.Benic dishonesty. Internet and Higher Education. 1999;2:21-34.

Ashworth P, Bannister P, Thorne P, Unit SotQRMC. Guilty in whose eyes? University students perceptions of cheating and plagiarism in academic work and assessment. Studies in Higher Education. 1997;22(2):187-203.

Bartlett J. Familiar quotations: a collection of passages, phrases, and proverbs traced to their sources in ancient and modern literature: Little, Brown, and company; 1904.

Barnhart RK, Steinmetz S. Chambers Dictionary of Etymology–the origins and development of over 25,000 English words. Chambers. Edinburgh, UK; 1988.

Cicutto L. Plagiarism: avoiding the peril in scientific writing. Chest. 2008 Feb;13

Conners M. Cybercheating: the Internet could become the newest battleground in academic fraud. The Muse. 1996.

College LHU. Undergraduate modular scheme (awards of the University of Liverpool)—appendices. 2012 [cited 2012 May, 15]; Available from: www.hope.ac.uk/compass/.

Dellavalle RP, Banks MA, Ellis JI. Frequently asked questions regarding self-plagiarism: How to avoid recycling fraud. J Am Acad Dermatol. 2007 Sep;57(3):527.

Fialkoff F. There's no excuse for plagiarism. Library Journal. 1993;118((17)):56.

Flint A, Clegg S, Macdonald R. Exploring staff perceptions of student plagiarism. Journal of further and higher education. 2006;30(02):145-56.

Harma BB, Singh V. Ethics in writing: Learning to stay away from plagiarism and scientific misconduct. Lung India. 2011 Apr;28(2):148-50. 24. Mason PR. Plagiarism in scientific publications. J Infect DevCtries. 2009;3(1):1-4.

Mallon T. Stolen words: Forays into the origins and ravages of plagiarism: Penguin Books; 1991.

Maurer H, Kappe F, Zaka B. Plagiarism-a survey. Journal of Universal Computer Science. 2006;12(8):1050-84.

Miziara ID. Ethics in scientific publications: the double copyright problem. Braz J Otorhinolaryngol. 2010 Sep-Oct. 76(5):543

Pyer H. Plagiarism. 2012 [cited 2012 May,16]; Available from: at: http://online.northumbria.ac.uk .

Sheard J, Dick M. Directions and Dimensions in Managing Cheating and Plagiarism of IT Students. 2012

CHAPTER V

Research Ethics and Plagiarism

Dr. Anjali Harangaonker

Associate Professor, Lakhmichand Institute of Technology, Bilaspur, Chhattisgarh.

E-mail: anjaliharangaonker15@gmail.com

Honesty is the best policy

Courtesy: www.tameyourassets.com/wp-content/uploads/2017/02/Depositphotos_40855487_m-2015.jpg

• • •

• • •

Research is a human endeavor. The word research is composed of two syllables -'re' and 'search'. The prefix "re" means a new or over again and the verb "search" means to understand, to investigate or to seek out. The term research refers to a process of systematic, methodical and ethical steps to solve a problem, to understand a phenomenon, to answer a question or to establish facts. Research is defined as the creation of new knowledge and/or the use of existing knowledge in a new and creative way so as to generate new concepts, methodologies, and understandings. This could include synthesis and analysis of previous research to the extent that it leads to new and creative outcomes. The primary purposes of basic research are documentation, discovery, interpretation, and the research and development (R&D) of methods and systems for the advancement of human knowledge. Research integrity is generally understood to mean the performance of research according to the highest standards of professionalism and rigor, in an ethically robust manner. Education, research, and innovation are basic pillars of contemporary advanced society. Research ethics are important for a number of reasons. They promote the aims of the research, such as expanding knowledge. They support the values required for collaborative work, such as mutual respect and fairness. This is essential because scientific research depends on collaboration between researchers and groups. A definition of research is used by **OECD Glossary of Statistical Terms**, "Any creative systematic activity is undertaken in order to increase the stock of knowledge, including knowledge of man, culture and society, and the use of this knowledge to devise new applications." Due to immense opportunities in innovation and increasing technological progress, trust in science lies in the trustworthiness of its researcher. Research is defined as careful consideration of study regarding a particular concern or problem using scientific methods. According to the American sociologist, **Earl Robert Babbie,** "Research is a systematic inquiry to describe, explain, predict, and control the observed phenomenon. It involves inductive and deductive methods."

Research ethics may be referred to as doing what is morally and legally right in research. They are actually norms for conduct that distinguish between right and wrong, and acceptable and unacceptable behavior. Researchers and students at various stages of their careers should receive instruction concerning conflict of interest, responsible authorship, data management, and sharing, as well as policies regarding the use of human and animal subjects. The literature review identifies flaws or holes in previous research which provides justification for the study. Often, a literature review is conducted in a given subject area before a research question is identified. A gap in the current literature, as identified by a researcher, then engenders a research question. The research question may be parallel to the hypothesis. Research can find answers to things that are unknown, filling gaps in knowledge and changing the way professionals work.

The word plagiarism comes from the Latin word 'plagiarized' which means to 'kidnap'. Plagiarism is defined as, "Plagiarism is presenting someone else's work or ideas as your own, with or without their consent, by incorporating it into your work without full acknowledgment."

In the age of ICT, huge resources of academic and research works are easily available to everyone through the internet. Plagiarism involves two things: taking other people's work (ideas, results, writings, and images) and presenting it as your own. Plagiarism is avoided by giving appropriate citations. Giving proper Citation adds value to our work: it shows that you have read literature that we know how the results fit together. Plagiarism is growing along with the increase of publications and academic papers. Plagiarism, specifically, is a term used to describe a practice that involves knowingly taking and using another person's work and claiming it, directly or indirectly, as your own.

SRP (Superfund Research Program) is committed to educating young researchers on these topics and battling the problem. We believe that the article contributes to raising awareness on the issue of plagiarism and that it can start new discussions among researchers and scientists Plagiarism is also regarded as unethical because when a researcher forwards somebody else's work as his own original work, it might be regarded as a kind of fraud. Plagiarism has been a problem in academic settings and appears to be on the increase, now moving into areas including the medical and scientific fields as well as industry, manufacturing, military and legal brief ethics in research is the most important component that one has to keep in mind while conducting one. It is very important to adhere to the ethical norms in research. The standard of conduct or the standard of behavior is reflected through the work of many authors. Plagiarism is becoming an increasingly large problem for publishers that require delicate handling. Recent conference surveys show an average of a dozen cases per robotics conference, and numerous cases have been initiated against authors for academic misconduct. Plagiarism is the act of passing off somebody else's ideas, thoughts, pictures, theories, words, or stories as your own. If a researcher plagiarizes the work of others, they are bringing into question the integrity, ethics, and trustworthiness of the sum total of his or her research. The peer-review process is the first line of defense against plagiarism and it is therefore important to raise awareness among students and professionals, to entirely understand the issue of (self) plagiarism, possible motivations should be identified. Researchers and scientists (in most countries) are evaluated on the basis of the number of publications, which has evolved into an important metric for assessing scientific merit. A consequence of this is publishing more and more for the sake of quantity, where quality takes second place. The objective of Research Ethics is to strive to avoid bias in experimental design, data analysis, data interpretation, peer review, personnel decisions, grant writing, expert testimony, and other aspects of research.

In 1999, the Committee on Publication Ethics (COPE) defined plagiarism as "Plagiarism ranges from the unreferenced use of others' published and unpublished ideas including research grant applications to submission under new authorship of a complex paper, sometimes in a different language. It may occur at any stage of planning, research, writing or publication; it applies to print and electronic versions" (Sharma & Verma, 2019). Plagiarism takes various forms. It can involve reusing an entire document, rewriting a single paragraph, or phrases or sentences without proper credit. Some information is considered common knowledge which means it doesn't need to be cited. Common knowledge is a kind of information that is widely known and easily verified. The consequences of plagiarism vary depending on the type of plagiarism and the context in which it occurs. In academia and other research-based professions, plagiarism has serious personal and professional consequences. An accusation of plagiarism can severely damage your reputation; it could result in loss. Plagiarism generally involves using other people's words or ideas without a proper citation but you can also plagiarize yourself. Self-plagiarism means reusing work that you have already published or submitted for publication. It can involve re-submitting an entire paper, copying or paraphrasing passages from your previous work, or recycling old data. Self-plagiarism misleads your readers by presenting old work as completely new and original. In case we want to include any text, ideas, or data that already appeared in a previous paper, we should always inform the reader of this by citing our own work or research funding and even our position.

Research is a derivative of the French word; 'Research' means quest, search, pursuit, and search for truth. Research in common parlance refers to a search for knowledge. It is a careful investigation or inquiry especially through the search for new facts in any branch of knowledge.

The main aim of the research is to find out the truth which is hidden and which has not been discovered yet. Though each research study has its own specific purpose; many more factors such as directives of the government, employment conditions, curiosity about new things, desire to understand causal relationships, social thinking and awakening, and the like may as well motivate (or at times compel) people to perform research operations.

Qualitative researchers have a dual mission to generate knowledge through rigorous research and to uphold ethical standards and principles. In enacting this dual mission, qualitative researchers might face ethical dilemmas that stem from the interpretive nature of qualitative inquiry. Given the emphasis that qualitative researchers place on holistic accounts, use of thick description, and presentation of raw interview and observation data, upholding participant confidentiality and privacy might be the most difficult challenge they face. When most people think of ethics (or morals), they think of rules for distinguishing between right and wrong. The term research ethics refers to a wide variety of values, norms, and institutional arrangements that help constitute and regulate scientific activities. The first two groups of ethical norms are internal, linked to the self-regulation of the research community; Research is a quest for new and improved or deeper insight. It is a systematic and socially organized activity governed by variously specific values.

'Ethics' is defined in terms of things acceptable and unacceptable or justification of what is right and what is wrong. Ethics is defined as the set of moral principles that govern a person's behavior or the conduct of an activity. People while studying or conducting research is perhaps ethically weak as they lose the standard of mind and conduct, to sense between what is right and wrong. There may be many reasons for the same but the idea of coping to such an extent that people have lost their imaginative skills as they are in the art of copying. Research ethics govern the standards of conduct for scientific researchers. It is important to adhere to ethical principles in order to protect the dignity, rights and welfare of research participants.

The ethical implications of plagiarism on self, aggrieved party, intended audience, and the community as a whole is the moral harm inflicted on all parties which damages the reputation of self and others, insults others' intelligence, and harms the integrity of all.

Ethics are the moral principles that a person must follow, irrespective of the place or time. Behaving ethically involves doing the right thing at the right time. Research ethics focus on the moral principles that researchers must follow in their respective fields of research. First, we must be committed to ethical principles. This means choosing an ethical behavior even if it delays our work or means of not getting published quickly in a prestigious journal. Although most people acquire their sense of right and wrong during childhood, moral development occurs throughout life and human beings pass through different stages of growth as they mature. Ethical norms are so ubiquitous that one might be tempted to regard them as simple commonsense. We should be responsible for all concerns related to your research. We should protect and safeguard all confidential information recorded in your research. Many different disciplines, institutions, and professions have standards of behavior that suit their particular aims and goals. These standards also help members of the discipline to coordinate their actions or activities and to establish the public trust in the discipline. People are more likely to fund a research project if they trust the quality and integrity of research. We should keep good records of research activities, such as data collection, research design, and correspondence with agencies or journals.

The development of search engines (such as Google) and open access storage facilities (YouTube) have created among users an expectation of universal availability, even a sense of entitlement to free access. As technology rushes ahead, the development of new legislation and business models is still in a state of flux. Another way of defining 'ethics' focuses on the disciplines that study standards of conduct, such as philosophy, theology, law, psychology, or sociology. Research often involves a great deal of cooperation and coordination among many people in different disciplines and institutions, ethical standards promote the values that are essential to collaborative work, such as trust, accountability, mutual respect, and fairness. We should ensure honesty in all forms of scientific communication with colleagues, sponsors, or the general public. It is important to evaluate the credibility of the information before making any decisions regarding research. Researchers need to ensure that they do not wield undue influence over others. Informed consent is a key principle of research ethics. It is important that the person who is invited to be a part of the research understands both the benefits and the risks involved. They must have all the information that could affect their decision to participate. Research is a multi-stage investigation leading to new insights, effectively shared. Research is a multi-stage process. Ethics are central to the research process. Researchers need to take care of various ethical issues at different levels of this process. The reality is there can be ethical concerns at every step of the research process. 'Turnitin' is a software that is meant to prevent the menace of plagiarism and ensure originality in the content. The official website of Turnitin says its software is a tool that helps "educators (and their students) make informed valuations". The principles of research integrities are to make research trustworthy, make research excellent, and underpin the positive impact of research, responsibility, and accountability in all aspects of research.

Ethical research is important for all people who conduct research projects or use and apply the results from research findings. All researchers should be familiar with the basic ethical principles and have up-to-date knowledge about policies and procedures designed to ensure the safety of research subjects and to prevent sloppy or irresponsible research, because ignorance of policies designed to protect research subjects is not considered a viable excuse for ethically questionable projects. Therefore, the duty lies with the researcher to seek out and fully understand the policies and theories designed to guarantee upstanding research practices.

The conclusion is that the act of stealing is not a true-crime; rather, it is the act of deception that inflicts moral harm on all parties by damaging the reputation of self and others, insulting others' intelligence, and harming the integrity of all. Plagiarism in any form is unacceptable and is considered a serious breach of professional conduct, with potentially severe ethical and legal consequences.

Research ethics govern the standards of conduct for scientific researchers. It is important to adhere to ethical principles in order to protect the dignity, rights, and welfare of research participants. Research ethics supports the values required for collaborative work, such as mutual respect and fairness. This is essential because scientific research depends on collaboration between researchers and groups. Ethics is a system of moral principles. They affect how people make decisions and lead their lives. Ethics are concerned with what is good for individuals and society and are also described as moral philosophy. To prevent Plagiarism there are several ways and resources but more than that it is the moral responsibility that one has to adhere to while undertaking such a project. The internet has sent shockwaves through the world of intellectual property; first in the music industry, then in all corners of publishing, in the image and film industry, etc.

Plagiarism is avoided by giving appropriate citations. Verbatim copying means using the same words as someone else, typically by 'cut and paste' should be avoided. Researchers face ethical challenges in all stages of the study, from design to reporting. These include anonymity, confidentiality, informed consent, researchers' potential impact on the participants, and vice versa. The basic aim and purpose of conducting research are to inculcate original thinking and analysis, but extensive copying and plagiarism counter such purpose. Given the importance of ethics for the conduct of research, it should come as no surprise that many different professional associations, government agencies, and universities have adopted specific codes, rules, and policies relating to research ethics. Many government agencies have ethics rules for funded researchers.

References

Neville, C 2007, „Introduction to Research and Research Methods", Bradford University-School of Management, viewed 11 November 2020, < www.brad.ac.uk/.../Introduction-to-Research-and-ResearchMethods.pdf.>.

University of Mumbai 2011, „Social Research-Introduction", viewed 15 November 2019, < www.mu.ac.in/ myweb_test/.../Research%20Methodology%20-%20IX.pd>

Singh, Y, K 2006, Fundamental of Research Methodology and Statistics, New Age International Publisher, New Delhi.

Smith JP. References, Copyright and Plagiarism (editorial). Journal of Advanced Nursing, 1997; 26(1):1.

CHAPTER VI

Academic Research and Publication Ethics

Dr. Vitthal Gore

Assistant Professor and Head, Department of English, Shri Havagiswami Mahavidyalaya, Udgir, Maharashtra.

Email: shmu2nptel@gmail.com

Be ethical, Follow the law

Courtesy: www.orvietocivica.files.wordpress.com/2018/08/ethical-legal-feature-1.jpg?w=768

• • •

• • •

As a researcher, academic research and publication ethics are expected to be followed. In fact, it is a burning issue of the present time. If an individual really looks at the entire academic research and publication scenario in our country, you will find that most of the research and publications have been a hidden treasure of the libraries. When we compare and contrast this scenario with the American, European and a few very top rated universities in the world; we will realize the status of research at the international front. So the present paper looks into the aspects related to academic research and publication ethics in general.

Research and publication ethics have to be followed in practical professional life. The title of this paper has two keywords – Academic Research and Publication Ethics. Whenever we look at research as a whole, it is found that any kind of research whether it is scientific research or else the research done in humanities or in any other domain of knowledge; it is a systematic investigation for pertinent information on a specific topic. For an academician, it is expected that when you are doing any research; it should be very systematic with a proper investigation for the pertinent information on the specific topic. In addition, it is expected to be very careful while doing an enquiry specifically through search for facts in any branch of knowledge that has been taken up for research. Sometimes a researcher really fails to talk about the facts, the kind of assumption that we have in the beginning and the conclusion that has been drawn at the end should justify each other. In between, a researcher is also expected to deal with some of the facts and reveal the facts to the person who is seeking knowledge from your research. So, in general one can say the kind of research that someone takes up is a kind of academic contribution from one's end to the existing stock of knowledge. A researcher always try his/her level best to make it for certain advancement in the domain knowledge because once the topic is taken up for systematic investigation, it will lead to certain conclusion. A researcher tries to retrieve the pertinent information as required for the specific part. S/he also finds out certain facts in this respect and tries to put forward these facts to somebody but beyond that as a whole one should look at the contribution which is an academic research contribution from the end of a researcher who will make certain advancement in the domain. It is actually a pursuit of truth and of course this is not only the pursuit of truth but a kind of pursuit of knowledge with the help of a systematic scientific study. A sort of observations that a researcher makes and undertake some of the experiments if at all the topic demands, and finally s/he comes to findings and conclusion but a holistic look at it, will bring out all kinds of academic research demands commitment, involvement and an approach that leads to some ethical issues into consideration.

Actually, the term 'ethics' itself is a very vast branch of knowledge that deals with moral principles and the values of a group of people of a community or society or state or country. Professionally culture and civilization are not going to deal with it; rather the topic deals with certain moral principles in your professional life. Sometimes we come across a person who is morally strong or s/he is very ethical in her/his practices. It means that the moral principles or values that s/he has cultivated and nurtured in the course of time are the part and parcel of one's personality. The moral values or principles, a set of ethical standards that someone adopts and adheres makes the foundation of professional life. But in the course of time, what happens with these moral values and principles actually govern an individual's behaviour and his/her own conduct. An ethically strong person will reflect the same in his personality. If someone is morally sound, it also reflects in the way s/he conducts any kind of activity.

These days the quality of research is degrading day by day. In the numerical point of view, it is showing vertical growth but in the qualitative point of view it is decreasing radically. So this is really a matter of worry for all the academicians and researchers. Ethics and moral principles are separate branches of study. They are treated as a part and branch of philosophy that involves systematizing and defending and recommending concepts of right and wrong behaviour.

When you try to correlate ethics or the philosophical world of ethics, you will realize that they refer to the rules provided by an external source. Do you think that the ethics are really introduced by an individual no matter whether they are cultural or social or professional values or the family values? It means these are the rules which are promoted or provided by the external sources and resources; so it is the responsibility of an individual who may be a teacher or academician or researcher to adopt the code of conduct in his/her workplace and be a principled kind of person as far as teaching and research is concerned.

When you generally talk about the field of ethics and try to correlate this with aesthetics; you will realize that the field of ethics along with aesthetics concerned the matters of value and enhances the values of an individual. It means the field of aesthetics comprises the branch of philosophy called axiology. Philosophy is an abstract realm, if you don't want to get into that but as a matter of fact without philosophy you cannot also live your own life.

Whenever we talk about ethics and values, I think we need to really consider certain codes of ethics. Now you can distinguish between what are the professional values and the personal values; once you are in a position to differentiate and distinguish between the personal and professional values then you will also have certain values called research values. Eventually, you come to a better understanding of distinguishing your personal life with the professional life. Whenever you talk about the code of ethics, you need to interrogate yourself when to take a stand on individual integrity, professional competence, confidentiality, objectivity, and professional behaviour. Now make an effort to dissociate the personal matters with the professional matters just try to separate it. Just try to dissociate by asking a question to yourself; what is the level of your integrity for the research activity, commitment, profession, competence and so on.

On this particular path of self-realization, improvement and development your professional competence will go up higher and higher. Similarly check your confidentiality when you work as a professional; as a researcher and how you really proved to be very objective and create a sort of objectivity in your own path of career. That will actually decide your professional behaviour altogether as a teacher, a researcher, and as an individual as well. If you correlate these things with your personal values and ethics and then your professional values and ethics automatically become the part of your personality which will grow day by day and your aura will automatically be realized by the people around.

Here an attempt has been made to discuss research ethics with the focused approach. As a matter of fact, what are we supposed to do; what are we supposed to remember; and what are we supposed to really follow and adhere in our personal life as a teacher, as a researcher and then you see the outcome will definitely be different as far as research ethics are concerned. All the research ethics that you really adopt in your personal academic research life whether you do a minor or major research project or PhD; we have a number of opportunities to involve these ethical values.

We undertake research projects, we have our own resources, we use multiple resources but now the question is how far you are committed for your own research and how far you are trustworthy while using various resources which are available at your desk because we are living in the highly sophisticated technologically advanced world. Already we have completed two decades of the 21st century; technology, Internet, computer, laptop, Smartphone, all these digital products have really made this entire word as a Global Village. The whole world is well connected with the help of Internet today, so e-content is available, e-resources are available but now the question is - how far we are trustworthy while using these resources and when you really see that somebody is very ethical about the use of resources automatically the outcome of research will also be equally good.

In addition, I will also discuss about the scientific misconduct and the kind of regulation which is introduced by the UGC that we have to follow while doing certain research and that is the reason that all of us are very careful about publishing our research papers in UGC Care Listed journals. We are very particular to see whether the journal is really doing the peer review process or not; we need to be so particular whether the researcher himself or herself has properly given justice to the topic or not. Actually, it makes a good researcher for the society, for the state, for the country. If you are ethically strong, automatically all these values will reflect in the kind of research that you undertake. Just to consider the research values is not sufficient; you need to actually adhere to these ethical principles in order to protect the dignity, and welfare of research participant. You might have heard about such kind of happening somewhere especially in the domain of science and technology that somebody has done research but unfortunately when the outcome is visible that a person is ignored and sidelined. He is not given any credit and automatically leads to the legal issue. The point is, these are personal codes of conduct; based on the respect for the self, others and all around. Unless it is really a very principled personality, how can others really expect from you that you will coordinate friendly and professionally to deal with the research matters.

Actually, several things are governed by the principles and assumptions underpinning the way individuals or organizations to conduct any research. A set of principles guide your research design and practice. Gradually an attempt has been made to discuss the core of research. So, these personal values and ethical values will be gradually continued with your research and academic values. So, the ethical considerations in research or any kind of research activity that you take up actually as a set of principles guide your research design and practices as well.

So, you have the research ethics which actually involve the application of fundamental ethical principles to research activities that you undertake. It also includes the design and implementation of certain research that you take up towards the society and others. It also provides you a platform to use the resources and the research outcomes by keeping in mind the kind of scientific conduct and misconduct you do and the regulation of research as imposed by the law of the nation for any apex body like University Grants Commission and so on.

Now try to understand, the goal of ethics in research. Gradually an effort is made to expand the boundaries of this discussion and definitely by the end you will be fully convinced that we have to have a very appropriate professional approach while dealing with these things.

So whenever you talk about the goal of ethics you need to really look into this matter that the goal of ethics in research is to guide the researcher to evaluate several things that you have - what the researcher is going to do in his research means what are they searching; what is the research project taken up for study; what is the objective of research; are hypothesis being tested in the best way; are protocol being followed as expected for the respective research; what is the study undertaken by the researcher. In the interest of society, you need to count it whether the lights of the respective subject are being protected by an individual or not. Unless the researcher is going to address all these goals, the research will never proceed.

Let's try to highlight a few research ethics and now you could see the research ethics as a whole. Everybody knows 'honesty is the best policy'. Now question yourself how honest you are to yourself; how honest are you to others; how honest are you for your profession; how honest are you while reading; while doing any kind of research, whether it is for a research article or for a major or a minor research project. Your own research, ethical, moral standards will reveal the fact and lets you know where you really stand.

Let's talk about the informed consent, sometimes we do follow; we do learn a few things from others and we do give credit to them in the respective document; at least they are referred to in the bibliography or else in the reference section; in the works cited section but if at all you are going to use somebody's scientific formula don't forget to take the proper concern from the Individual; don't forget to give him the credit; don't forget to involve the person into your research activity. Similarly, be very ethical as far as beneficiaries are concerned; be very particular about the non-magnification of the person's identity; be very responsible for the kind of publications that you use because if at all you are getting benefit from.

We should be open minded and the most important thing in the research field is you should give due respect to the intellectual property rights.

Never get into the legalities, if at all you are not giving due respect to the intellectual property rights; may be a lateral stage you may be into a difficulty. How do you really justify your own research work and while giving credit to certain people, you are using their material, using their references, using their content, whether you are following the rules and regulations especially provided in the IPR and whether you are really conscious of plagiarism.

The United States of America has a unit called National Science Foundation and they have defined types of misconduct in 3 different categories what are these categories number

1. Fabrication
2. Falsifications
3. Plagiarisms

As far as the fabrication is concerned, it means making up the data or result; it means doing some sort of fabrication with either the data or the results which are actually the outcome of some other research; whereas you have falsification means to manipulating the research material. The research process or changing or omitting the data or the results which are the outcomes of the previous research done by somebody else and here you falsify the things such as the research is not accurately represented in the research record. It means all together you proved to be a kind falsified personality or a personality who has created some sort of falsification in the process of research. No one should ever fabricate, never falsify, never plagiarise. Plagiarism is presenting someone else work or the ideas as your own it means you claim that actually something belongs to somebody else but you claimed that this is your research outcome.

As far as intellectual honesty is concerned intellectual honesty in proposing, performing, and reporting research which actually referred to the honesty with respect to the meaning of one's own research. If you are intellectually honest, you will never falsify the matter; if you are intellectually honest, you will never fabricate the matter; if you are honest, you will never like plagiarism because these things are interconnected and of course it is expected that the researcher present in the proposal and the data honestly. If at all it is your own, s/he will claim that it is his own and he will communicate the best understanding of the work in writing and sometimes in verbal form also if at all needed when you develop your research paper, when you develop your thesis, when you write your thesis, you are responsible for everything.

References

Nimish Choudhary and Sara Hussain (2021) *Handbook of Research and Publication Ethics*, Bharti publications, New Delhi.

https://www.who.int/activities/ensuring-ethical-standards-and-procedures-for-research-with-human-beings

https://www.stir.ac.uk/research

https://www.apa.org/monitor/jan03/principles

https://www.scribbr.com/methodology/research-ethics/

https://www.ncbi.nlm.nih.gov/pmc/articles/PMC4196023/

https://www.publichealthnotes.com/research-ethics-definition-principles-and-advantages/

Ethical Issues in Research: An Observation

Dr. Sanjay Trimabkrao Haibatpure

Associate Professor and Head, Department of English, Pandit Deendayal Upadhyaya Mahavidyalaya, Deoni, Dist. Latur, M.S.

E Mail ID: <u>*haibatpuresanjay@gmail.com*</u>

Ethics make you confident

Courtesy: <u>https://s3-us-west-2.amazonaws.com/courses-images/wp-content/uploads/sites/4052/2019/04/10172441/ethics-2110558_1920-e1554917143920.jpg</u>

• • •

• • •

The subject of research about ethics is significant now, not as it was when conducting research, but moreover when publishing it. It is one of the significant columns for keeping up logical keenness and validity. Of course, it is an intellectual activity. It nurtures to execute reasonable practices lies with researchers, universities/institutions, and publishers.

Ethics are broadly the set of rules, or regulations written and unwritten, that monitor our needs of our have and others' conduct and behaviour while conducting professionally. They are the ethical rules that regulate a person's conduct. Research approximately ethics may be suggested to as doing what is morally and really right in and around roughly. They are really benchmarks for conduct that recognize between right and wrong, and palatable and unsuitable conduct.

Research is a multi-stage process. Ethics are central to the research process. Researchers need to take care of various ethical issues at different levels of this process. The reality is there can be ethical concerns at every step of the research process as pointed out by Bickman and Rog (2009).

Effectively, they set out how we expect others to act, and why. Though there is a deep understanding on a number of ethical and moral values, there is as well a wide assortment on how accurately these values ought to be deciphered in practice.

Through this paper, we expected to supply a brief however comprehensive asset to graduate understudies and early-stage analysts. We have recognized common regions where analysts frequently confront questions and challenges. We have shared bits of knowledge on well-known themes such as how to dole out creation, how to dodge picture control and plagiarism, how to oversee inquire about information successfully, or how to distinguish clashes of interface.

What is ethical conduct of inquiry about? You'll have frequently listened to the term "ethics." It is by and large characterized as a set of standards that recognize between worthy and unsatisfactory behaviour or way of conducting an errand. These rules or standards may shift over nations, disciplines, educate, and indeed research facilities. For occasion, these morals may not as it were direct the conduct and working of an organization or a government but moreover a trade substance! Do you know which codes you ought to take after when conducting your research?

First of all, these ethical codes not as it were offer assistance to keep up logical keenness but to protect the essential point of conducting an inquiry about i.e. to advance information and truth. Furthermore, these values advance belief, regard, and objectivity in a collaborative work environment by dodging clashes related to creation, copyrights, and others. In addition, these codes offer assistance to keep up the security and intrigues of human subjects and guarantee fitting care of creature subjects in a clinical or research facility setting. In conclusion, these moral standards make analysts responsible for the quality and result of the inquiry about and that will straightforwardly or in a roundabout way influence open wellbeing and interface.

Different organizations have played an instrumental part within the advancement and appropriation of the ethical rules over colleges, universities, publishers, and teaching. A few of the unmistakable names are recorded underneath. In addition, colleges and research institutes set up a free authoritative substance called Ethical Committee (EC) or an Institutional Review Board (IRB).

Research ethics are the set of ethics that oversee how consistent and other research about is performed at colleges, and how it is spread. This paper explicates more around research morals, and how you will be able to do research about and lodge a complaint. In spite of overseeing for the foremost portion with human and animal individuals, unmistakable branches of social sciences deal with unmistakable techniques and ethical issues. Other than choices to be taught by shared values and experiences, ethical and moral conducts may engage the researcher's personal judgments in development to the capable ethics.

Let's see, what are research ethics? When most individuals think of research ethics, they think almost issues that emerge when investigate includes human or creature subjects. Whereas these issues are in fact a key portion to investigate ethics, there are more extensive issues approximate benchmarks of conduct. These join the centrality of disseminating disclosures in a direct way, not replicating others' work, and not tainting work.

Amid the study or research, Indian researchers have to be passed on most extraordinary significance to the social contrasts, and cultural milieu of the country. They must work inside a system appropriate for all the traditions, conventions, languages, castes, logic, colours, classes, locales, etc. They must work for the movements of all the social orders, religions, etc., not the other way circular. Amid the research about, the researchers must be beyond any doubt the wide conservative, information and innovative crevice between the individuals of India.

Indian colleges, universities and academic institute explore ethical committees. Researchers have no other elective but to depend on their claim common sense to allocate with and minimize differing basic ethical issues. Along these lines, required for a common approach or a common system both at private as well as national level making a distinction Indian researcher in tending to the ethical issues is cardinal.

As there is a differentiate interior the nature of issues rising completely distinctive methods of ask almost, all the colleges and universities in India must be organized with ethical committees at the departmental level or workforce level. Investigate conventions may be submitted to such committees for thought, course, modify and endorsing many times. These committees may offer assistance to advance the mindfulness with respect to the do's and don'ts. The committees may act as the go between and advisor in wrangled about issues.

The ethical issues have appeared up an increment with an approach in improvement, as seen, these committees may give direct on all such things. Such ethical committees may lock in an organizational explore culture based upon solid benchmarks. These committees must be committed to tall quality, clear and careful ask around ethics all through India. The committees may also screen the advancement of the progressing considers. On the other side, the researcher may also overhaul the committees with respect to the occasions and issues and status.

Research ethics are basic for a number of reasons. They back the centers of investigate nearly, such as common or collaborative attempt. They back the values required for collaborative work, such as common regard and tolerability. Regularly essential since consistent ask around depends on collaboration between examiners and bunches. They mean that researchers can be held tried and true for their activities.

Researchers should require the sole commitment for the moral conduct. In basic terms, arranged to say ethics are researcher's commitment. To begin with and the preeminent obligation of an examiner is to require care of the security, respectability, rights and well-being of the individuals. Researchers need to take care of assorted other issues at arranged stages of investigation. Both the researcher and people have a basic role to play. One's rights are the other's commitments. Researcher should watch out of the participants' rights and must consider from participants' point of view.

Government offices look at regularly spread codes of conduct for researches, or codes of ethics. Various or in reality most moral codes cover the taking after zones: genuineness and judgment recommends basically have to be to report your look at really, which this applies to your strategies (what you did), your information, whether you've got as of now disseminated any of it. You got to not make up any information, checking extrapolating absurdly from a number of your attempts roughly, or do anything which may conceivably be deciphered as endeavouring to sell out anybody. It is transcendent to undersell than over-exaggerate your revelations. When working with others, you need to tirelessly keep to any understanding, and act sincerely.

The researcher should point to sidestep incline in any viewpoint of your ask approximately around, checking organize, information examination, clarification, and peer ponder. For case, the researcher got to never underwrite as a peer commentator a few individuals you know, or who have got worked with, and you have to endeavour to guarantee that no bunches are by chance denied from you explore. This as well proposes that you just basically got to be uncover any individual or cash related interface which can affect you inquire about around.

The researcher should ceaselessly be arranged to share your information and comes approximately, close to any cutting-edge gadgets simply reasonable have made, after you scatter your revelations, as this makes a differentiate to engage information and development science. You should also be open to feedback and display day contemplations.

The researcher should be never fitting or duplicate other people's work and try to pass it off as you have done it. You got to ceaselessly ask for consent some time as of late utilizing other people's gadgets or techniques, unpublished information or comes around. Not doing so is academic theft. Clearly, you'd like to regard copyrights and licenses, adjacent to other shapes of mental property, and determinedly recognize commitments to examine roughly. Inside the event that in address, recognize, to sidestep any threat of scholarly robbery. You've got to regard anything that has been given in certainty.

The researcher should convey to progression to state of research and information, and not sensible to progress your career. This proposes, in centre, merely basically reasonable need to not disseminate anything that's not progressed, or that copies somebody else's work. You have to ceaselessly take care of laws and headings that control your work. On the off chance that you're utilizing creatures in your look at, you have to be ceaselessly being past any address that your tests are both significant and well-designed. You got to as well appear up regard for the animals you're utilizing, and make past any address that they are truly cared for. In case your inquiry about individuals, you ought to make any address merely essentially reduce any conceivable hurt to the scarcest, and expand the benefits both to people and other individuals.

This gathers, for case, basically need to not uncover individuals to more tests than are totally pivotal to fulfill your look at focuses. You need to ceaselessly regard human rights, tallying the assurance and independence. Keep in judgment aptitudes that the Ethics Code joins particular commands for examiners who conduct exploratory treatment investigate. Particularly, they must admonish people around the test nature of the treatment, organizations that will or will not be open to control bunches, how people will be entrusted to drugs and control bunches, open treatment choices and compensate or budgetary costs of participation.

Regulatory actions by UGC and the science departments, whereas attempted with the most excellent conceivable eagerly, led to at slightest two terrible results within the Indian context:

1) Careless application of bibliometrics while deciding appointments, promotions, and awards. There is now the distressing trend of appointing and rewarding people merely because they have publications in high impact factor journals. A pedestrian 'follower' paper from India can appear in a high impact factor journal for various reasons, including but not limited to the patronage sometimes extended by a First World referee towards an author from the Global South, a sense of unwritten obligation as it were, or a tendency to 'allow' an Indian follower in the same field to publish in a high impact factor journal if he/she cites a big 'leader' scientist from the First World. Such a 'leader' may well be the referee; the Indian paper gets published but it is never cited. Such 'follower' papers from the Global South will not be cited where it really matters.

Indian committees for appointments, assessments or awards at the Central Government level often go, sadly enough, by impact factor of the publication journals of candidates. These committees are necessarily of a general composition. They cannot be expected to go into the finer but more crucial details of the candidates' research to discriminate between truly insightful and adequately competent work. It is not a surprise therefore that average academics get elevated to positions of authority in India because it is normally only the receipt of such awards that elevates one to such positions.

2) Policy makers and administrators worldwide have been concerned for some time that research is being paid for twice over: the first time when it is funded and the second time when journal subscriptions are paid. Scientists should not be charged twice — once to undertake research and then to view its outcomes. This has led to the appearance of a new type of journal, the Open Access (OA) publication. In an OA journal, an author pays a one-time fee to publish a paper. Subsequently, its access is open to anyone. So, if a government funding agency earmarks a certain amount (say 15 per cent) of a research grant towards OA fees, it would pay for research just once. The OA model has been successful and excellent OA journals now exist. The model has been widely adopted by European governments and there is a little doubt that India should follow this path, because it is the future (UGC, 2-3).

Other steps researchers have to take to consolidate: Conversation approximately the limits of puzzle. Provide people data around how their information will be utilized, what will be done with outline materials, photographs and sound and video recordings, and secure their consent. Know government and state law. Know the ins and outs of state and government law that might apply to your look at.

Another illustration is that, whereas most states since it were require authorized clinicians to comply with mandatory enumerating laws, some of laws also require investigators to report abuse and overlook. That's why it's essential for investigators to coordinate for circumstances in which they may learn of such reportable offenses. By and sweeping, examine nearly investigators can direct with a clinician or their institution's legal division to choose the first astonishing course of action.

Take practical security measures. Be past any question any address private records are put truant in a secure amplify with restricted get to, and consider stripping them of recognizing data, on the off chance that doable. As well, use caution of circumstances where assurance may incidentally be breached, such as having secret discussions in a room that's not soundproof or putting participants' names on bills paid by accounting departments.

India is no exception and to get to the root of the matter, we must appreciate the complex and diverse higher education system in India. The University Grants Commission (UGC) is a statutory organization established by the Government of India (GoI) for the coordination, determination, and maintenance of standards of teaching, examination, and research in university education. India has over 40,000 colleges providing undergraduate courses and over 900 universities focused on postgraduate education and research.

According to the data of 2019-20 of the All India Survey on Higher Education (AISHE), about 1.503 million teachers were present in the system at that time to train 38.56 million students, of which 4.312 million were in the Master's programmes and 202,550 in doctoral programmes. During 2019, about 38,986 students were awarded Ph.D. degrees. The GoI awards nearly 10,000 research fellowships every year. According to Scopus data, about 147,537 articles were published from India. Majority of the research articles published are contributed from over 100 institutes of national importance and from a large number of national laboratories managed through different research councils. Historically, a typical Indian affiliating university caters to degree education, whereas the national institutes and laboratories are focused on research. Except in a few cases, this bifurcation seems to be a major reason for the poor research culture in most Indian universities.

Responsible conduct of research, and safeguarding ethics and academic integrity in scientific research is extremely crucial. Compromised publication ethics and deteriorating academic integrity are contaminating all domains of research. Unethical, deceptive practices in publishing have led to an increased number of dubious/predatory journals worldwide. In India, the percentage of research articles published in predatory journals is high. It is important to prevent academic misconduct, including plagiarism, in academic writing among student, faculty, researcher, and staff. The Indian academic community needs to ensure that the journals/conferences it chooses to publish follow standard ethical policies (UGC, 5).

Think around information sharing some time as of late ask almost nearly starts. On the off chance that examiners organize to share their information with others, they have to note that interior the assent handle, appearing how they will be shared and whether information will be shrouded. For outline, investigators may have burden sharing unsteady information they've collected in a think roughly of grown-ups with veritable mental sufferings since they fizzled to explore people for authorization to share the information. Or formative information collected on tape may be a profitable asset for sharing, but unless a researcher's consent back at that point to share tapes, it would be beguiling to do so. When sharing, examiners need to utilize built up procedures when conceivable to secure riddle, such as coding information to cover up personalities.

Get it the limits of the internet. Since Web innovation is persistently progressing, clinicians ought to be imaginatively savvy to conduct examine online and cautious when exchanging mystery data electronically.

In this paper, we investigated the estimations of an ethical ask almost. We as well came to memorize around the commitments a researcher has towards the people in specific and society in common. We inspected the do's and don'ts of an ethical ask around roughly. Isolated from the common ethics, the paper moreover analyses the ethical issues analysts in India must be past any address in spite of the fact that conducting ask around nearly. Through this paper, we as well support the foundation of examine ethical committees at the departmental level in each college and university across India.

References

Bickman, L., & Rog, D. (2009). Applied Research Design: A Practical Approach. In L. Bickman & D. Rog (Eds.), Handbook of applied social research methods (2nd ed., pp. 3–43). Thousand Oaks, CA: Sage.

WEB ACADEMIC INTEGRITY AND RESEARCH QUALITY, UGC, New Delhi, 2021.

www.ugc.ac.in/ebook/Academic%20and%20Research%20Book_

CHAPTER VIII

Online Educational Resources Must Safeguard the Core Credits of the Creators

Dr. Divya Maheshwari

Associate Professor, Tolani Commerce College, Adipur, Dist. Kachchh, Gujarat.

Email: drmaheshwari512@gmail.com

OER: Techological Blessing in disguise

Courtesy: OERDefinitionGraphic.png   https://www.k12.wa.us/sites/default/files/

• • •

• • •

Online Education Resources, briefly known as OERs, relate to a digital technology through which one initiates the overall learning to experience whereas Plagiarism means someone incorporates the idea of the other in one's own original without full acknowledgement of its real originator.

The universal role of educational system is to promote learning which leads to creativity, innovations and researches. But sometimes the reality of rote-learning and cut-copy-paste dominate the world of originality. This practice of plagiarism weakens the fulfillment of the aims of the educational system, especially when the stakeholders in a particular field surrender to Plagiarism. As plagiarism is due to the acts of marginalization rather than of mission; the educational system should alert itself against such interferences and should focus on the efforts that curtail the weakening aspects like plagiarism. For eliminating the inferences, an emphasis on objective-achieving features should be strengthened in such a way that its barriers remain auto-rejected.

At least educational system, not sometimes and somewhere but always and everywhere, should strictly reward innovative ideas and practices instead of allowing the rote learned ones. Of course, OER must be under an intellectual property license with the permission for free use or free from plagiarism, following the netiquette ethics and the Intellectual Property Rights (IPR) should be properly protected for having much more significance in many areas.

Change in Educational Modes: A Requisite

The present reality in the field of education is knocking at the door of the learning campus for updating the generations with the fact that the conventional classroom teaching, and especially transmissive lectures, were planned for another age and now a different era requires different methods for the key shift with more focus on skills, chiefly knowledge management, and less on rote learning. Here, mentoring needs design models that lead to the development of the required skills needed in a digital age of education, the design models for teaching that are light and nimble that can operate in most cases as well online as in class.

Managing the Digital Education Scenario

Teaching in a Digital Age is a general overview of online teaching and learning. Faculty are facing unprecedented change, with often larger classes, more diverse students, demands for more accountability and above all, all have to cope with ever changing technology. To handle change of this nature, teachers and instructors need a base of theory and knowledge that will provide a solid foundation for their teaching, no matter what changes or pressures they face. Although our institutions will need to change for healthy survival by maintaining and strengthening their core values. It is important to manage the change, protecting the core values rather than throwing out everything and starting something fresh!

Online Educational Resources: One of the Changes

OERs belong to digital technology that can be considered as one of the most important changes in the field of education, freely available over the Web or the Internet. OERs are permitted digitized materials for educators, students, and self-learners under a Creative Commons (or other "open") authorization which allows its users their use for educational and research purposes. OERs provide a platform to learn according to one's own pace and to have quick access to all the latest information. These include learning matters such as syllabi, curricula, reading, lecture material, simulations, experiments and demonstrations, thus, they help all in personalizing the overall learning experience.

History of OERs

Once Online Educational Resources were presented to the education world in 2002. In the subsequent ages, as added organizations and institutes started Open Publishing Programs, and Creative Commons began its licensing platform to certify and kick-start the open licensed model. Then OERs were seen as an effective way to ensure that all students, regardless of economic status, had the resources they needed to succeed. Today, the evidence is starting to mount that OERs really can have a positive impact on the educational system, from K-12 through postgraduate programs.

Present Status of OERs

OERs are active initiatives at colleges and universities around the world.

- Over 150 universities in China participate in the China Open Resources for Education initiative, with over 450 courses online.
- Eleven universities in France the Paris Tech OCW Project, offering over 130 courses.
- Seven universities in Japan, the Japanese OCW Alliance offer over 140 courses.
- Seven universities in the United States with OER projects offer over 1400 courses.

Altogether there are over 2000 freely available university courses currently online. Moreover OER projects are emerging at universities in other countries also. There are also several translation efforts underway to broaden the impact of OER initiatives. The number of non-course OERs available is exploding as well. Rice's Connexions Project currently hosts over 2,700 open learning objects (http://cnx.rice.edu) available for mixing and matching into study units.

Textbook Revolution (http://textbookrevolution.org) contains links to hundreds of freely available, copyright clean textbooks. Freely accessible encyclopedias like Wikipedia (http://wikipedia.org) and Math World (http://mathworld.wolfram.com) grow in size and quality. Thus, the momentum behind OER is clearly building.

Trends in OER Development

- Many OER projects at universities and colleges are beginning at the "bottom", being driven by faculty rather than administration. There is even an example of a project being driven by the students within a university (http://ocw.hampshire.edu/).
- Most OER projects are using Creative Commons Licenses (http://creativecommons.org) or the GNU Freed Documentation License (http://www.gnu.org/licenses/fdl.html) to license their content.
- Projects like eGranary (http://www.widernet.org/digitalLibrary) and the open source Edu Commons software (http://educommons.sourceforge.net) are making it easier than ever to mirror open educational resources for use in settings where connections to the Internet are slow, expensive, and / or unreliable.
- Podcasting, screen casting, and video casting are becoming increasingly popular as inexpensive ways to capture and distribute course content
- Folksonomic approaches to creating metadata and indexing ("free tagging")

OERs are gaining their popularity with end users (e.g., see http://del.icio.us or http://flickr.com). In brief, the general public along with the teachers and students access the OERs primarily to enhance their personal knowledge, to plan or prepare a course or learn about topics related to their research and to plan their course of study.

Usage of OERs

These accessible resources support the corporate learners multiply their knowledge and expand their understanding of specific topics or tasks. E-Learning specialists can also practice OERs to enrich their online training courses, even if they are pushed for time and on a tight corporate eLearning budget. One can use these by substantiating Usage Rights, by safeguarding that Online Resources Pass the Quality Assurance Test, by generating an Open Educational Resource and by repurposing the resources to create courses with a wide-range. This particular digital technology is important for many reasons as mentioned below.

Significance of Online Educational Resources

As OERs became increasingly available during the 2000s and have continued to expand worldwide, higher education institutions began to adopt OERs into their courses - even offering "zero textbook" classes. Open Educational Resources are budget-friendly, easily reachable, readily accessible resources and are free for the masses.

These OERs hint at the present educational needs to move from a transmission model of education ('instruction') to the facilitation of learning ('teaching'), even or especially in post-secondary education. Here, as OERs can play its significant role to boost the facilitation-morale for teaching-learning stakeholders as are freely accessible, openly licensed text, media, and other digital assets that are useful for teaching, learning, and assessing, as well as for research purposes with quick and fast speed. There are different types of OERs such as Open Courseware, Learning Modules, Open Textbooks, Streaming Videos, Open Access Journals, Online Tutorials, Digital Learning Objects, etc.

Five Rs of OER

In order to encourage educators to clinch the openness of OERs, a framework was established, known as the 5Rs, to define the rights of open content and provide guidance on how to use these resources.

1. Remember: Make own copies of the resource indefinitely.
2. Recycle: use the resource in a variety of ways.
3. Review: Adapt, modify and improve the resource.
4. Reproduce: Combine the resource with other resources to create a new work
5. Reorganize: Share the resource with others.

OERs Are Cost Effective

Primarily, many academic stakeholders, and others advocated for the use of OERs in higher education because of the cost savings for students and families that open resources offered.

Advantages of OERs

a. Engrossed by pioneering faculty, the educators began acclimatizing OERs for their drives, creating original course content that involved and engaged students in ways that textbook reading and practice did not.
b. Instructors began to assess the materials and learning outcomes of their courses in a more careful manner because they now had freedom to familiarize, amend, and relate those resources in a more targeted way.

Disadvantages of OERs

What is unethical is not borrowing itself but borrowing without acknowledgement. OERs implicate seriously, especially in professional and academic situations if something is plagiarized illegally. Even if this has been done accidentally, it is still classed as plagiarism if one tries and claims that somebody else's words or ideas are one's own.

Magnetisms for Plagiarism

One side plagiarism is broadcasted badly but on the other side some super-intelligent plagiarists love it. Plagiarism contains some magnetic powers. For example: Just one picks the content from someone else and makes its own and earns credit – it's that easy.

Plagiarism Is Unethical

Plagiarism is unethical, immoral and evil because someone is intentionally copying stuff from another source to claim it as one's own. The cost of plagiarism can be particular, professional, principled, and permissible. It is critical to avoid plagiarism as it upsets one's reliability. Moreover, plagiarism takes away the credit that the unique one justifies and could end up in a legal battle if legal action is taken. Here are some strategies to practice plagiarism-free research. So, avoiding plagiarism is necessary to attract more innovative ideas.

Strategies to Practice Plagiarism-Free Research

So as to evade plagiarism in your research paper, consider the points given below:

One should always...

i. Mention the sources that one practices.

ii. Quote the quotations.
iii. Interpret judiciously.
iv. To bring fore more meaningfully own original ideas.
 v. Practice a trustworthy plagiarism-checkers

Along with plagiarism checkers, there are some other ways to control unethical practice of plagiarism. These are known as Intellectual Property Rights.

Plagiarism Vs. Intellectual Property

Intellectual Property (IP) denotes the conceptions of the concentration, a brand, origination, literary and artistic works, design, names and images used in commerce or other kind of creation and it is owned as legal rights over them by a person or business. In order to harness originality with an objective to enable innovations grow, a reliable IP framework is the best option.

IP Environment in India

The Intellectual Property India is administered by the Office of the Controller General of Patents, Designs and Trade Marks (CGPDTM). This is a subsidiary office of the Government of India and administers the Indian Law of Patents, Designs, Trade Marks and Geographical Indications.

India's Intellectual Property (IP) legislation covers every significant aspect of the protection of IP. Although Indian IP law is thorough and generally comparable with European IP laws, there are still significant concerns over IP enforcement. A major cause for concern in enforcement is bureaucratic delay, with a backlog of cases at both the civil and criminal courts. This means that cases can run for five years or more. There is also a lack of transparency, particularly at a local level. A noteworthy article of the IP milieu in India is the large number of small players overstepping IP rights. This means that captures tend to be small, which requires a nonstop and financially strenuous effort in order to make an effect.

Anyway, it is essential to know how to use, guard and enforce the rights one has over the Intellectual Property (IP) that one owns. To enjoy most types of Intellectual Property (IP) rights in India, one should register as any unauthorized use of a subject of an intellectual property right represents its harm.

The most important way to avoid problems when defending IP rights in India is to be prepared. To make sure that one can anticipate any potential issues, one should seek take advice from Indian IP rights experts from other experts. For example lawyers, local diplomatic posts, Chambers of Commerce and the Business Council at an early stage on how to protect one's IP.

Intellectual Property Rights

Intellectual Property Rights (IPR) are the legal rights given to the creator to protect her/his invention or creation for a certain period of time. These legal rights confer an exclusive right to the inventor/creator or her/his assignee to fully utilize his invention/creation for a given period of time.

The most common IPRs include patents, copyrights, marks and trade secrets. It is very well settled that IP play a vital role in the modern economy. Thus, any originality of innovator should never be credited to others who are original plagiarists, not innovators otherwise real can be disappointed and the plagiarist can be awarded which is anyway not practicable for maintaining the ethics.

Need for IPR Enforcement

Intellectual Property Rights play an important role in promoting innovation and protecting investment, particularly in the digital and green economy. Enforcement of IPR implies the application of efficient and proportionate administrative civil measures and penalties by competent authorities against those involved in counterfeiting and piracy. Strong and enforced Intellectual Property Rights protect consumers and families, ensure products are authentic, and of the high-quality that consumers recognize and expect. IPR foster the confidence and mental peace that consumers demand and markets rely on. Therefore, an efficient and effectively enforced intellectual property infrastructure is necessary to ensure the stimulation of investment in innovation and to avoid commercial-scale Intellectual Property Rights (IPR) infringements that result in economic harm.

Conclusion

Online Educational Resources should be used with required etiquettes promote respect for the creators and copyright holders of online content. Educationists need a strong basis for measuring the worth of diverse technologies, innovative or prevailing, and for determining how or when these technologies make sense for them to use. Intellectual property protection is critical to fostering research, innovation and scientific development in a country like India. Without safety of ideas, concepts, and research; individuals would not gain the full advantages of their research and inventions. Since India is one of the fastest developing countries, we need to focus on basic research, scientific rights are worth defending, both and technological development. Thus, IPRs are very significant role players both ways, nationally and internationally.

References

Intellectual Property and Copyright Ethics," Business and Professional Ethics Journal, 10.2 (1991): 85-109. Reprinted in Robert A. Larmer (Ed.), Ethics in the Workplace, Minneapolis, MN: West Publishing Company, 1996, 278-293.

Glasgow L J. Stretching the limits of intellectual property rights: Has the pharmaceutical industry gone too far? IDEA J Law Technol. 2001;41:227–58. [Google Scholar]

Steeves, V. (2014). Young Canadians in a Wired World, Phase III: Life Online. Ottawa: MediaSmarts, pp. 35-36. http://mediasmarts.ca/ycww/life-online

Dennis Carter. The top 10 ways college students plagiarize. eCampus News, May 15, 2012.

http://www.ecampusnews.com/top-news/college-plagiarism-students-682/

Organization for Economic Co-operation and Development' Centre for Educational Research and

Innovation. Expert Meeting on Open Educational Resources, David Wiley, Utah State University Centre for Open and Sustainable Learning.MIT OCW's 2005 Evaluation Report. https://www.oecd.org 11 Oct., 2021

Why OER? Business Open Educational Resources and Fair Use: MURRAY STATE UNIVERSITY,

University Libraries https://libguides.murraystate.edu

Fundamental Change in Education https://edisciplinas.usp.br>mod>book>view

Teaching in Digital Age- Open Collections https://open.library.ubc.ca>media>download>html

Challenges and Problems in Research Pertaining to Current Scenario in Tamil Nadu: A Practical Approach

Dr. K. Subapriya

Assistant Professor, PG and Research Department of English, Pachaiyappa's College, Chennai, Tamilnadu.

E.mail: dr.subapriyakannan@gmail.com

Ehtical Search for Research

Courtesy: https://s3-us-west-2.amazonaws.com/courses-images/wp-content/uploads/sites/855/2016/10/17193458/17664002728_acb9354acf_z.jpg

• • •

• • •

When UGC has passed a rule that PhD/NET/SET is mandatory to become a qualified Assistant Professor, the demand for PhD has increased. Every Tom and Dick is in search of PhD vacancies. At the same time, UGC has laid restrictions on the vacancy for the aspiring professors. An Assistant Professor could take only four researchers to guide and on the other hand an Associate Professor could supervise six researchers. It is a welcome move from UGC since its main was to maintain the quality in research. Previously, professors of all grades were allowed to supervise in 10 researchers. However due to the restrictions enrolling of students for research in fake universities and deemed universities has gone high. Due to the pressure people register for PhD in some other district and state where eventually the contact between the guide and the researcher will be variably less. The researchers are somehow in a hurry to get a PhD degree for their employment and it eventually affects the quality of research.

Surpassing all these number of seats available, yet another common problem that one could see among the aspiring researcher approach for a PhD seat is that they have a broad idea about the topic but they lack any idea about the exploratory research. Even to arrive at a particular topic of thesis, it is better for every researcher to do exploratory research. The Concise Wardswarth Handbook gives a good deal of knowledge about how to do this exploratory research. The exploratory research done in a proper way will lead to the pathway of focused research. It is best explained through the following diagram,

Exploratory Research

Pathway of Exploratory Research

Most of the scholars have trouble in locating the research gap and the lacuna to arrive at the problem of the thesis. The best way to address this issue is exploratory research. Once when the broader topic is decided, to nail down on the particular topic, one has to refer to online catalogue, library shelves and general reference works. Through culling out these three sources, research questions can be arrived at. By tracing and examining the research questions, primary questions for the focused research can be found out. To do elaborate focused research, again one has to refer various primary and secondary sources like books, articles, specialized reference works, data base internet, interviews and surveys. An additional advantage is that interviews and surveys will make the research more factual and livelier.

The above listed strategy has to be duly followed before drawing a broad outline for the thesis structure. Mapping an outline and using the index card or documenting the collected secondary sources in any form of electronic gadgets is yet another important criterion to carry out a proper research and documentation without any confusion. There will be much vain when one tries to collect the title of the article, journal, volume number, date of publication, date of downloading, URL and publisher after citing the author's opinion in the content of the thesis.

Nowadays, smart work is considered as better than hard work. Best search engines to locate the secondary sources should be used by the scholars to reduce the time and energy. Some of the best popular search engines are Ebscohost, Expanded Academic ASAP, First Search, Readers' Guide to periodical literature and ERIC, etc. Researchers can effectively make use of the above listed search engine to make their research more profound and effective.

To evade the problems in research methodology and to have more knowledge in research ethics, course like M.Phil. was also initiated. Its main aim was to promote the basic idea about how to pursue research. A separate paper on research methodology and criticism becomes the major part of M.Phil. Curriculum. However, recently UGC has scrapped this M.Phil. and in contrary Government of Tamilnadu still insists to retain the M.Phil. course to provide the basic idea of research. Therefore, M.Phil. course at its best still functions in the research department of colleges and state universities to provide the ground work for research. A student is transformed into a research scholar during this M.Phil. course and he/she is introduced to the MLA style and other research methodologies. It is like undergoing small research training before entering into the actual research of PhD program. The universities have made provisions to include papers on research methodology and subject area for those who opt for direct enrolment to Ph.D. after PG. It is a welcome initiative as the knowledge on research methodology and ethics is mandatory for every researcher.

No wonder, this paper on research methodology further equips researcher on how to record some information through summarizing, paraphrasing or quoting. During this process of research, when no proper summarizing, paraphrasing or quoting is done, intentionally or unintentionally researchers tend to fall in the line of plagiarism. Plagiarism, the word itself has become more popular and a well-known term. One could come across this term even in the text book of a fifth-grade student. Plagiarism is defined as "presenting another's idea, information, expressions or entire work as one's own. It is thus a kind of fraud: deceiving others to gain something of value" (MLA 8th Edition 3). Recently many steps have been taken by universities and UGC which has put a check on plagiarism, especially in case of the submission of research thesis as plagiarism is always considered as a serious and ethical offense. The Universities have introduced the usage of software to check and present the percentage plagiarized content. A candidate will be allowed to submit his/her thesis only after receiving the due certificate signed by the technical person from the particular section. There is also yet another question whether this method is strictly followed in all the universities of India without any relaxation or discrepancies.

Advantages of Plagiarism Software

1. It ensures the promotion of authentic research work.

2. Quality of the research is enhanced.

Disadvantages of Plagiarism Software

1. At times even the formulas or quotes in case of textual based research, and all the other universal data is accounted as Plagiarism. Though certain amount of plagiarism is accepted considering this problem, still every time the researcher has to take due care about this in order to keep his/her thesis within the plagiarism limit.

2. Software fails in recognizing the materials drawn from age old text which is available only in print form. This sort of plagiarism may not be spotted through the software.

3. A pre-trial of the document to check plagiarism leads to the devastation of 100% during the actual process of plagiarism checking at the university premise.

Apart from this plagiarism software issues, one of the most significant problems encountered is the constitution of the examiner panel. The forthcoming paragraphs will throw more light on those issues.

Discrepancies in Examiner Constitution

Throughout India, uniformity is not followed in constituting the examiner panel. Some universities award Ph.D. degrees based on the report given by Indian examiners alone while some insists on three-member panel including Foreign, Indian and Regional examiners. The discrepancies in this model have lot of negative impact. Especially a variety of problems are faced in case of finding and processing a thesis towards a foreign examiner. The problems are listed below,

1. Most of the foreign examiners especially Europeans and Americans are

reluctant as the remuneration offered is meager. The remuneration does not reach them on time.

2. Getting a report from the foreign examiner and processing a thesis towards viva takes more time. In many universities there is no such process at all. So, those research candidates finish it quickly and receive their degrees while a few university research candidates' theses gets stagnated for many years and they are denied earning their degree and job on time. It is a great mental agony for the research scholars.

3. It takes immense time for the process of thesis, during which foreign examiners who give their consent either change the institution or refuse to evaluate as the consent given time has evaded.

4. Tracing foreign examiners for a new research field is very difficult. Insisting to submit a foreign panel comprising three experts with the publication dating back only to the recent five years of the submission is a great challenge for the guide. Thereby, both the research guide and the candidates turn hesitant to explore a new field.

5. University demands the foreign examiners who have publication in UGC Care list journals. As UGC Care Listed journals are repeatedly revised, when the panel is submitted, the article will be in UGC Care List but during the process of forwarding thesis, the journal may be removed from the list and naturally the panel gets rejected.

6. The article of the panel experts is compared exactly with the title of the thesis thereby providing an article of the expert related to the thesis area or the author is never taken into consideration. The panel should be accessed by the subject experts, only then the concept and ideology will be understood and the panel will get approved.

7. In case of humanities, their style is different and thesis writing is highly put to dispute. They have a different methodology. Moreover, they always operate under the umbrella term humanities and expertise in various other fields also contributes to different fields but their affiliation is not approved in panel.

The universities and academic bodies should evolve a common methodology in examining the thesis process to ensure the justification of quality and the quantity of research produced. It is high time to take necessary steps to protect the welfare of the research scholars.

Yet another problem faced by research scholar is the mandatory rule that insist the scholars to have publication in at least two UGC Care Listed Journals. The proposal to submit a Publication in UGC Care List was laid to enhance the research quality by UGC but in reality, the scenario is quite different. No open submissions could be done in UGC approved journals. The submissions are done indirectly through someone. Heavy charges are laid even for good research papers. Scholars are somehow forced to pay the charges as they have to move for the submission of thesis. The quality ensuring process is well used with business strategies to mint money.

Despite the problems of an individual research scholar and the ambiguity caused due to the existing rules and regulations, one has to remain ardent in pursuing their research. Research done with interest and passion no doubt will yield joy, pleasure and fruitful results. Certain steps should be taken from the administration and academician side to ensure quality research. A panel of academicians and researchers can be constituted to check the pros and cons of the rules and regulations imposed upon in a regular duration. Opinions and data collected from the guides and researchers should be given due importance to do away the hurdles in research progress and submission process. After the trial-and-error method, rules can be brought into practice.

References

The Concise Wadswarth Handbook. Eds. Laurie G. Kirszner and Stephen R. Mandell. United States: Thomas Advantage Books, 2005. Print.

"How to Write a Thesis Statement". Indiana University Bloomington. 22 Sep, 2021. https://wts.indiana.edu/writing-guides/how-to-write-a-thesis-statement.html

MLA, 8th Edition: Daytona State College. MLA, 8th Edition: An Introduction and Overview. August 2016. 23 Sep, 2021. https://daytonastate.edu/cwc/files/Codex-MLA8.pdf

Plagiarism and Research Ethics. Eds. Mark Valters and Franko Vivaldi. 15 Nov, 2018. Downloaded 22 Sep, 2021. http://www.maths.qmul.ac.uk/~fvivaldi/teaching/rmms/plagiarism.pdf

Stone, Sue. "Humanities Scholars: Information Needs and Uses". Journal of Documentation. Vol 38 (4). https://www.emerald.com/insight/content/doi/10.1108/eb026734/full/html

CHAPTER X

Higher Education in India: Itself a Research Potential Sector

Dr. Kulkarni Sanjay Ganpatrao

Assistant Professor, Department of English, Netaji Subhash chandra Bose College, Nanded, M.S.

Email ID: sgknsb@gmail.com

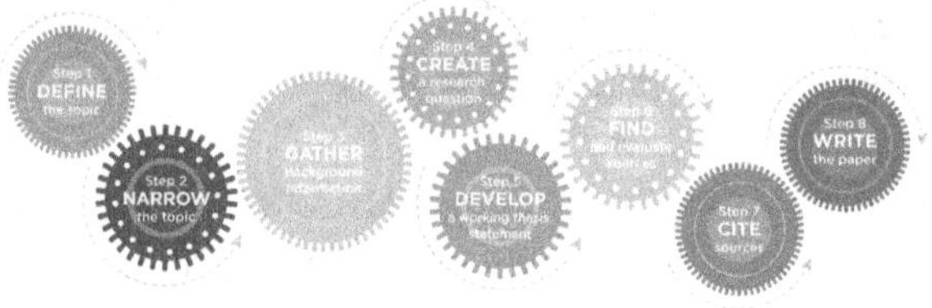

Research demads a process

Courtesy:www.s3-us-west-2.amazonaws.com/courses-images/wp-content/uploads/sites/106/2016/07/30185522/Research-process-8-gear-final.png

• • •

• • •

Indian Higher Education is the third largest in the world after China and United States in terms of Enrolment. However, in terms of quality, Indian higher education has still to pass many tests to meet with the global competence. There appears an endless list of Indians facing problems with higher education system. The present Higher Education system of India is producing graduates that are without employability skills. The standard of academic research is near to the ground. If we look at the imbalanced teacher-student ratio, rigid academic structure, improper obligation of subject options, interference of politics in education sector, corruption, lack of innovations and inadequate sources of public funding are some of its decisive problems. Due to such numerous system deficiencies, higher education system of India is suffering a lot. There are various and distinct issues which decide the status and strength of the Nation. Irrespective of all these problems, our education system plays an important role in the status of our nation at the international front and equally contributes to the economic growth.

Objectives

1. To investigate different Problems and obstacles of higher education in India
2. To investigate the challenges and opportunities of higher education in India

With above aims and objectives the researcher intents to write this paper in order to take self-comprehensive review of the Indian higher education system and study its need by identifying the gaps for the bright future of our upcoming generations. Looking at the present scenario of the higher education in India, an attempt has been made to study it critically and comprehensively. At the outset, if we look at the research-oriented initiatives in higher education, we may say that the real system of higher education in India was implemented by the British to serve their economic, political and administrative interests. But after the independence, higher education system has been expanded tremendously. If we look at the structure of Higher Education System it consists of 282 private universities, 123 institutions as well as 367 state and 47 central universities. (Indian Higher Education in Transition, IJES, Vol.1, Issue3, Jan-2015)

MHRD has taken many initiatives to achieve the objective of quality, equity and accessibility. So National Knowledge Commission in 2006 recommended that there is a need to focus on quantity and quality of Higher Education. National Knowledge Commission also reports on major areas of concern like expansion and accessibility of higher education, governance and administration, contents in terms of curriculum and examinations and regulatory framework, institutional architecture of universities, financing and in the faculty and research. The most important issue tried to solve with the help of the research-oriented initiatives are like RUSA (Rashtriya Uchchatar Shikshan Abhiyan), INFLIBNET (Information and Library Network), NAD (National Academic Depository), IMPRESS (Impactful Policy in Social Sciences), MHRD Initiatives on Promotion of Research and Innovations, and Shodhganga, e-Shodh Sindhu, STRIDE and Swayam Prabha, etc. In this way Innovation has become synonymous with evolution and progress in life. Education is the only way to effectively train the population not only to benefit from the exploits and fruits of innovation but also to actively participate and contribute to this crusade for creating a better, safer and healthier planet.

When we look at the barriers and challenges in higher education; it is our duty to solve the problem of gender inequality because it is found in all sectors. Gender is a social construct that impact attitude, roles, responsibilities and behavior patterns of girls and boys, men and women in all societies. Education sector is one of the affected areas where we see inequality. Female participation in Higher Education is less progressive particularly in the rural areas in the present era. Somehow the literacy rate shows progressive form but what is the reality? Even today, girls have been facing barriers while taking education. It is because of poverty, social, cultural norms and practices, poor infrastructure, violence and fragility. She is constructed by the society needs. Her image, her life is not her own but it is designed by male dominated society. Gender discrimination, child marriage, Dowry system, feeling of insecurity and parents' psychology are the major reasons that throw her out from the educational system. In this way all knowledge is within the human mind and education is the only way to recover it. Hence, Swami Vivekananda very rightly said, "To educate your women first and leave them to themselves, they will tell you what reforms are necessary". But what we see, that is different condition of women related to her education. The Urban female literacy rate is 64 percent and rural women literacy rate is hale of it. In our India many states have large rural-urban differences in female literacy. (Dalmia & Lawrence).

If we try to look at the changing dimensions of Higher Education then the role of education has been the key factor of human progress. Without education human society cannot sustain itself in a good manner. Though education has a long and hard history the purpose of acquiring knowledge has changed as per the change in time. Not long ago, education was the driving force for intellectual prosperity but today it has become the means of sustainability. The time is not far away, when education will be the only thing that can keep humans alive. Therefore, it can say that the dimensions of education have changed significantly in a very short span of time. The same thing has been explained with the help of time. In the past, education is used for 'Brain' but at present, education used for 'Bread'. Similar to this, in future, education will be used for 'Breath. (Singh P.R.)

There are many challenges before Indian higher education system. The present system is based on traditional or general education where the students only get their degrees but they don't get their dignity. The problem of unemployment is very crucial. The Indian universities and colleges are not able to provide market driven courses and thus it is felt that Indian higher education is no longer 'productive one'. Apart from employability there are some serious issues like equity, access, relevance and quality in higher education.

In our critical study if we look at purpose of this paper, it can be said that in our higher education many major issues are there. At present, India is facing basic problems in higher education. These include inadequate infrastructure and facilities, large vacancies in faculty positions, poor faculty, low student enrolment rate, out dated teaching methods, declining research standards, unmotivated students, overcrowded classrooms and widespread geographic, income, gender and ethnic imbalances. Apart from these deteriorating standards, there is reported exploitation of students by many private players. Ensuring equitable access to quality higher education for students coming from poor families is a major challenge. Students from poor background are not academically prepared to crack highly competitive entrance examinations that have bias towards urban elite and rich students having access to private tuitions and coaching. Education in basic sciences and subjects that are not market friendly has suffered a lot.

Research in Higher Education institutions is at its lowest ebb. There is an inadequate and diminishing financial support for higher education from the government and society. Many colleges established in rural areas are non-viable, are under-enrolled and have extremely poor infrastructure and facilities with just a few teachers. There is an absence of a well-informed reform agenda for higher education in the country. A few efforts made now and then are not rooted in the new global realities based on competition and increased mobility of students and work force.

Based on observations, some remedies are suggested for improving higher education in India. The foremost need of making drastic changes in the higher education is need of interlinking the enrollment ratio of students with the number of colleges and universities in the country. Infrastructure is required in a huge number to cope up with the competition of many private and foreign universities in India. A great deal of effort is also required for creating value for education. Today there is more and more requirement of skills based and industry-oriented education for creating employment opportunities. Expected changes in Higher Education are such as:

1. Skill based education,
2. Vocational courses,
3. Industry-college/university linkages,
4. Self-Employment short term courses, and
5. Extensive use of technology in higher education.

Conclusion

At last, to conclude, it reminds us of Swami Vivekananda who said, "Education is the manifestation of the perfection already in man." It means, Education is the effective way to make the life progressive and changeable. It is like a strong weapon to overcome the calamities which impact upon our life. It helps us to improve our life in a better way. Education certainly determines the quality of an individual's life. Education improves our skill, knowledge, personality and attitude. It helps us to find out the needs and limitations of our life. It enables us to express our thoughts and views. It also increases our innovative thoughts. Higher Education is the vital part of any economy. The growth and the development of any country depend upon the development of human resource of that country. The human development is also very crucial in developing the society and bringing harmony in the world. Therefore, the modern methods of teaching, learning, evaluation, research and employment generation are required in a great number. This responsibility lies upon the shoulders of higher education in our India. Hence, I strongly suggest that Higher Education in India itself has a great potential for research. Committed researchers should get into this realm and suggest the government to improve quality, equity with equality.

References

Dalmia, S., & Lawrence, P., The Institution of dowry in India: Why it continues to prevail. The Journal of Developing Areas, 38(2)

Govt. of India, MHRD, All India survey on Higher Education portal, 2018

Higher Education in India, Issues, concerns & New Directions http://www.ugc.ac/in/publneindia.pdf.

Indian Higher Education in Transition, IJES, Vol. 1, Issue 3, Jan. 2015.

Kurup, M.R., Quality of Higher Education: Impediments and Initiatives, University news, 2010

Ministry of Human Research Development.2013, New Delhi: Govt. of India, Rashtriya Uchchatar Shiksha Abhiyan.

Neetu Rathore. *A Study on Empowerment of Women in India.* International Journal of Engineering Technology Science and Research IJETSR www.ijetsr.comISSN 2394 – 3386 Volume 4, Issue 11 November 2017.

Prasad, Ramesh, Indian Higher Education in Transition, IJES, Vol.1, Issue3, Jan.-2015.

Singh, P.R., Challenges in Higher Education in India: An Analysis, IJSSR, Vol.2, April-2016.

Swami Vivekananda. https://thesanatanchronicle.com/2020/08/30/brahmavadini-the-forgotten-tradition-of-women-scholars-in-ancient-india/

Swami Vivekananda. https://vivekavani.com/education-manifestation-perfection-man

CHAPTER XI

Basic Principles and Strategies to do a Plagiarism free Research

Ms. J.D. Sampale

Assistant Professor, Department of English, Shri Havagiswami Mahavidyalaya, Udgir, Maharashtra.

Email: sampale.jyoti@gmail.com

Say No To Cut, Copy and Paste

Courtesy: https://www.nbcnews.com/id/wbna32657885

• • •

• • •

Plagiarism means to present someone else's concepts or ideas without giving any acknowledgement to the creator or without giving any credit to the creator. It is an academic misconduct of representing other's ideas as your own and not mentioning the original source. The main purpose of research is to add or discover or invent new ideas which will enhance the existing stock of knowledge. Plagiarism encourages original research and stop the tendency of merely copying or presenting other's ideas. This paper mainly discusses the foundational principles of Plagiarism and the strategies to avoid this unethical practice while conducting research in various academic disciplines.

Plagiarism is an act of directly or indirectly copying/quoting/paraphrasing other's ideas as your own without mentioning or using the source. It is a kind of offence and liable for punishment under the intellectual copy right laws. It is always good to be careful of citing and mentioning the source of the content in a proper methodology and ethical ways. Commonly plagiarism occurs in many ways like direct plagiarism, self-plagiarism, accidental plagiarism, complete plagiarism and patchwork plagiarism. In the world of digital technology, it is easier to detect plagiarism. New researchers must know about it and take steps to prevent it.

Basic Principles of Plagiarism

Plagiarism matters concerning the following attributes. Here are a few specific principles of plagiarism that matters in academic and research arena.

Understanding the wider knowledge

True purpose of education is to enhance the understanding of life and the world and this is possible only when a researcher studies deeply about the particular subject. True research invents new possibilities and ideas hence benefit truly for betterment of mankind. Academic research is an intellectual challenge, if someone completes it successfully; it will benefit in order to understand the topic fully and this way one can achieve the purpose of research.

Growth of human knowledge

The broad purpose of research is to add and build new ideas reconsidering the earlier contributions by researchers. Plagiarism presents merely others' ideas and not so beneficial for the societal issues and expected solutions. Research must to add some value and not merely presenting earlier contributions in the new form. Advancement of human knowledge is possible through the promotion of plagiarism free academic research only.

Academic Integrity

To maintain academic integrity, plagiarism matters. It is essential to represent academic works, studies, and findings about a particular topic truthfully. Plagiarism fosters true academic work and stop unethical practices. Academic integrity mentions to the practice of adopting ethical ways to carry out research. It is always fair to have academic integrity in research work. Plagiarism free research shows an academic integrity hence research work gives the contributor a sense of pride.

Acknowledgement of Creator's Credit

A basic principle of scholarly research is that scholars deserve credit for their contributions, their ideas and intellectual toil; henceforth the credit must be acknowledged legibly. If someone is using the creator's new ideas erasing his or her acknowledgment, it will discourage or underestimate the original ideas. It will be like discouraging the creation and so it may harm creativity. It is very much necessary to attribute the credit to the original creator.

Intellectual property Rights

Intellectual property Rights (IPR) refers to the creation of the mind such as inventions, literary and artistic works. IPR provide protection for creation and inventions to enable creators to earn recognition and financial benefit from their work. IPR is a right given to a person for the creations of his or her minds. IPR usually gives the creator an exclusive right over the use of his/her creation for a certain period of time. The main motive of intellectual property rights and related issues is to promote and reward inventive research. Above all, the principles depict clearly why plagiarism matters in academic writing and how it is important to use ethical approach while conducting your research.

Strategies to avoid plagiarism

There are many online plagiarism checking tools and platforms. One can use these tools and platforms and keep oneself away from this unethical practice. Here are a few ways to avoid plagiarism in your research:

1. Properly cite and acknowledge the sources
2. Include quotations properly
3. Properly paraphrase the content
4. Present your own ideas

5. Use online plagiarism tools
6. Keep a track of the sources in your research
7. Not to procrastinate with your research, as good research takes time.
8. Allow bounteous time for in-depth understanding of the topic
9. Record bibliography accurately.

Plagiarism free research can be done if a researcher takes care of these things as stated above.

Plagiarism Prevention Blueprint

One must consider the following blueprint while doing scholarly work -

* Use quotations when taking someone's exact words
* Paraphrase while using someone's ideas in your own words
* Use citations while taking ideas from a source
* Follow the rules of citation style
* Prevent of Self-plagiarism
* Use of reliable plagiarism checker
* Use of reference list for every source
* Think alike a scholar to prevent plagiarism

An academic researcher is a scholar who thinks practically and studies in detail to resolute societal issues through his/her research.

Conclusion

The main motive of any research is the creation of new knowledge or addition to the existing standard of knowledge in a unique and creative way for enriching the present stock of knowledge. Research must be completely plagiarism free so as to promote creativity and innovation. The principles discussed in this paper can help all the researchers to understand the reason why plagiarism matters in research works. These principles will definitely help a researcher to conduct research ethically and follows the legible ways hence ultimately it makes the research work truthful and trustworthy. When you carry your academic work in this manner, it becomes more meaningful and resolute. Undoubtedly plagiarism free research is the voice and valuable contribution to the society.

References

https://carleton.edu>writing
http://classic.austlii.edu.au
https://www.anzela.edu.au